VAMPIRO

Portrait of a vampire bat ready to spring into action. Photo by Bruce Hayward.

VAMPIRO

The Vampire Bat in Fact and Fantasy

~ ~ ~ ~ ~ ~ ~ ~

by

David E. Brown

~ ~ ~ ~ ~ ~ ~ ~

~ ~ ~ ~ ~ ~ ~ ~

Drawings and Maps by Randy Babb

~ ~ ~ ~ ~ ~ ~ ~

~ ~ ~ ~ ~ ~ ~ ~

High-Lonesome Books
Silver City, New Mexico
88062

~ ~ ~ ~ ~ ~ ~ ~

ISBN # 0-944383-22-X

Library of Congress Catalog Card # 94-75838

~ ~ ~ ~ ~ ~ ~ ~

~ ~ ~ ~ ~ ~ ~ ~

DEDICATION

To the memory of Alvar Nuñez Cabeza de Vaca who wrote down all
that he observed and then some

Front cover photo by Randy Babb

Back cover photo courtesy of the Eastman Kodak Company

FOREWORD

For more than thirty years, biologists have expressed a concern about declining populations of bats on a worldwide basis. There are a number of aesthetic reasons for this distress, ranging from the loss of biodiversity to a missed opportunity to witness a nectar-feeding bat drinking from a hummingbird feeder on someone's back porch. But aesthetic concerns alone will not benefit bats in that these mammals do not elicit feelings of warmth and coziness as do the cute little squirrels and big brown-eyed deer that we protect in our parks. Fortunately, to the naive question, "what good are bats to man?" there are a multitude of answers from agricultural economics to medical research on human infertility.

Most people are unaware of the practical benefits of bats, nor do they know much of anything about bats. An "informed" enthusiast will ask about bat radar not knowing that these animals possess no such thing. That people are ignorant about bats is evident to me whenever I hold a live bat to show to an audience, and two questions inevitably are asked. To the first, I reply, yes, it will bite; mammals have teeth to process food and to defend themselves. And to the second question I say, no, the animal at hand is not a baby bat, you just expected it to be larger because of the false impression that people have regarding the size of these little animals.

But while the public lacks accurate information on bats in general, their dearth of knowledge pales into insignificance when compared to what they think they know about vampire bats. After all, people having been told all about vampire bats in a ceaseless well-spring of horror films, science fiction novels, and campfire stories -- the only problem being that from little to none of this information is factual.

Now Dave Brown gives us a reprieve from myth and ignorance with his book, *Vampiro*. Although written for the non-biologist, even bat-specialists will appreciate Brown's synthesis of the published work on vampire bats, his review of their biology, the summary of methods used to control these parasitic mammals, and the curious details of the legends regarding non-bat vampires (or as Brown calls them, vampyres, to differentiate the real bats from these human superstitions).

I was mesmerized by the first vampire bat I held. He had big dark eyes and I was enamored of him even as he tried to slice into my hand. But Brown does not try to convince the reader, as I might, that these are merely one of nature's wonderful creatures, the product of evolution to a very different lifestyle that selected for the most marvelous adaptation of drinking blood. Rather, his account about vampire bats is honest. He gives equal time to the vampire bat-borne diseases and the economic hardships that these animals have wrecked upon man and his animals.

Now, the reader finally learns the truths about vampire bats. He or she will learn that primitive peoples adjusted to these animals while modern man plods determinedly ahead, teasing these bats with a new and ready food supply, his domestic livestock. The result we see is yet another example of the problems man creates with the introduction of non-native species. Here, in the New World, these introductions have permitted a species of bat to increase in numbers, and in turn, to increase their scourge. This relationship is in fact what drew Brown to write about these bats. For, while many bat species are declining due to man's disturbance, the common species of vampire bat is thriving.

Brown explains the ecologically significant results that have come about, through the cooperative research of agencies in the U.S. and hispanic countries in joint attempts to develop successful control programs for vampire bats, without destroying more beneficial species of bats in the process.

I wish vampire bats still occurred here in the southwestern U.S., as their fossils remind us they once did before being excluded by climatic changes. What a wonderful animal for observation by both the biologist and avid naturalist! But if vampire bats had still occured in the U.S. in recent time, they surely would have met the same fate as our Mexican wolves and grizzlies. In anger we would have attemted to exterminate them in *our* thirst for blood. But then, perhaps as Dave Brown suggests, *el vampiro* would have survived our wooden stakes.

Ronnie Sidner
Bat Biologist, University of Arizona

CONTENTS

LIST OF ILLUSTRATIONS

PREFACE

I have always had a romantic fascination with lands to the south. This intrigue was doubtlessly influenced by my boyhood readings of Spanish conquistadors, South American rubber barons, Indian chicle gatherers, and MacAmerican filibusters. Later, as my interest in natural history grew, I learned about other tropical adventurers and the wonderful discoveries of Alexander von Humboldt, Charles Darwin, and William Beebe. Even today, Theodore Roosevelt's exploration of Brazil's "River of Doubt" remains in my mind as the ultimate achievement of an American president who just also happened to be my country's foremost conservationist. Where else but in the American tropics could one come upon such bizarre creatures as cave-dwelling oil-birds, huge electric fishes, avian fossils with claws on their wings, ants that advanced in military columns like panzer division, and fishes that were said to "strip the flesh from a floundering horse in minutes."

My early fascination was reinforced when I later had the opportunity to see some of these phenomena for myself. Who can visit a rain forest and not be stunned by the abundance and diversity of life found therein? Even in the Neotropic's driest regions, every tree or cactus seems to come in a different form and shape. Each bird outrivals the next in colorful plumage and melodious song. The mammals too, possess a wonderful array of spots, stripes, and hues, and make up for any lack of numbers by their endless variety of shapes and sizes. As for reptiles and amphibians, the New World tropics boasts a collection of deadly and harmless denizens rivaled by few other places on earth. Boreal animals, by way of contrast, while larger in size and numbers, are few in species and almost uniformly dull in color.

Moreover, the people are friendly and helpful; each morning is bright and sunny and the air filled with bird noises. The villages smell of burros and the day's meal cooking on some exotic wood. Brightly flowered flamboyant trees punctuate the roadsides, and every house has a red tiled roof, a dog, a parrot, and too many children. The women have those dark flirtatious eyes which turn the most casual glance into a whispered promise. Soon, within days, even the most casual visitor is inflicted with the contagious fever that makes tomorrow less important than today.

Not that the tropics don't have their downside. But then were it not for risk and discomfort, there would be neither romance nor adventure. The heat of the day can nearly smother you, and may persist into the night in a miasma of stillness that threatens to drive you mad. Chiggers, gnats, mosquitos, ants, and other biting insects are there to annoy you in endless forms and numbers. Venomous snakes

1

lurk in the undergrowth, and the threat of Chagas' disease, malaria, and a myriad of other tropical ailments are always present. Even the plants have the power to sting, poison, and irritate you. One of the most unusual of these dangers, I had heard, were vampire bats, winged demons said to subsist entirely on the fresh blood of mammals that they visited in the dead of night. Not only were these creatures capable of surreptitiously purloining your blood, they sometimes transmitted fatal diseases in the process -- diseases fatal to not only man's livestock but to man himself.

Although I had long been aware of vampire bats, I did not have an opportunity to see their work until a visit to Costa Rica's Guanacaste Province in 1986. Leaving my travel-weary wife in San Jose, I made a foray to Palo Verde National Wildlife Refuge on the Rio Tempisque to see what manner of waterfowl wintered there. My quest fulfilled, I had left the refuge late the following day when I came upon a ranch and corral south of the town of Bagaces. Here something caught my eye. Streamers of dried blood were clearly evident on the necks of several zebu-like cattle gathered within the twisted logs of the corral. What or who, I wondered, had inflicted so much sanguinary damage. Had the animals been attacked by a *tigre*?

The ranchmen leaning over the corral soon set me straight. What I was looking at *senor*, was the work of *vampiros*. Their ravages had been particularly troublesome this year. The rains were late and the dry weather seemed to have brought the bats out with an increased vengeance. Or maybe it was just that the rains had begun. The men themselves appeared to disagree as to why so many of their cattle had been bitten. My Spanish was too poor to follow their explanations other than that the weather was somehow to blame.

Wanting to see these goblins of the night for myself I contacted Dr. Lendell Cockrum, Arizona's resident bat expert, on my return to the states. Not only did Dr. Cockrum have a few vampire bat tales of his own to relate, he showed me a number of specimens housed in the University of Arizona collection. One of the skins of a common vampire was labeled as collected in 1959 at Minas Nuevas, the site of an abandoned mine just a few miles from Alamos, Sonora. Alamos had been a silver mining town since Spanish colonial times and was only 300 miles south of the Arizona border. He also told me that the U.S. government was hard at work getting rid of vampire bats, and that some ingenious methods had been devised for their destruction. I had arrived in Arizona too late to see wolves and grizzly bears. Was I now to miss out on vampire bats as well?

Such was not to be the case. Vampire bats are still to be found in good numbers, not only near Alamos, but almost throughout their extensive range. All one needs to meet a vampire bat is an experienced bat-catcher. Fortunately Arizona has some of the best. Two of them,

2

Randy Babb and Barry Spicer, are good friends of mine and readily agreed to participate in a vampire-bagging venture. Besides being interested in all things pertaining to natural history, Randy is a herpetologist, and he and some friends had spent the last three summer vacations camping near Alamos at a trailer park called El Caracol looking for reptiles to photograph and collecting insects. He also had netted bats there, and in the summer of 1991, he had been bitten by a vampire bat that he had caught. Barry, besides being one of Arizona's bat experts, is fluent in Spanish. Accompanied by two other veterans of Randy's Alamos excursions, Pete Mayne and Spanish-speaking Karen Galindo, we set off on an expedition in search of *los vampiros*. One could not wish for more competent and compatible companions.

Despite selecting a dark and moonless night as we had been advised to, our attempt to net vampire bats at Aduana where Randy had caught his tormentor of the year before was a bust. Although such nocturnal strangers as bull-dog bats, funnel-eared bats, and even a naked-backed bat, found their way into our mist nets, no *vampiros* were to be had. The highlight of the night was instead a piercing scream that not only silenced the nightly practice of Aduana's musicians, but the village dogs as well. Clearly someone was being brutally murdered at the old mines in the hills above the village. Instead, that someone was me, and the scream was my reaction to being bitten by one of several bulldog bats which had become entangled in the net. In my haste to release these unwanted prisoners unharmed, I foolishly removed a glove to better grasp the net, and had inadvertently brushed against one of my frightened captives. My scream was not so much from the pain as from surprise and agitation over the bat's escape. His unwelcome departure insured that I was in for a series of antirabies shots on my return to Arizona.

Regrouping the next morning, we made a visit to the Asociación Ganadera in Alamos to seek local expertise. Nor were we disappointed. Thanks to Karen's diplomacy and fluency in Spanish, our odd request to learn of *el vampiro's* hideouts was accepted without derision. Furthermore, the lady in charge, Concepción Nieblas de Acosta was most helpful, and introduced us to a veterinarian, Ernesto Alcorn. Ernesto had recently participated in a local vampire bat control program and thought he could show us some mine shafts inhabited by these animals.

Later that afternoon, guided by Ernesto, we visited the abandoned silver mines above Minas Nuevas. The site certainly looked promising. A naked hill of eroded mine tailings, looking like a heap of bleached bones, guarded the approach to the mines. As we clambered over ancient walls, overgrown with brush, we came upon the brick skeletons of buildings. The mines themselves were tunnels of various angles leading down into the bowels of the mountain which had long

3

been divested of its treasures. Certainly such an eerie place was haunted by vampire bats. Not wanting to descend into the gloom of the mine, and possible disturb any bats before we could ply our nets, we decided to forego further explorations of the mine's interior until the morrow. Instead, we would return tonight to try our luck with José Maria Miranda, another veterinarian who had also generously agreed to accompany us.

Late that afternoon, well before sunset, we set our mist nets. Three were placed in front of horizontal tunnels, while another was set over a vertical shaft near the hill's summit. As a further precaution we set two of the longer nets along likely looking flyways through the scrubby forest. It was good that we had an early start, as these chores were not as easy as we first envisioned. Much chopping and clearing of vegetation was required to insure that the nets were set low enough to the ground to catch our prey. Nonetheless, dusk saw our task accomplished as we took our respective stations to eagerly await the arrival of Ernest, José Maria, and *los vampiros*.

We don't have long to wait, for either our new comrades or the evening contingent of bats. No sooner has darkness crept over our increasingly spooky surroundings, then we catch our first bat -- a *Glossophaga soricena* at 7:20 pm. A dog barks from the *pueblo* below and soon afterwards we see Ernesto's and José Maria's flashlights bobbing through the underbrush. Bats of various shapes and sizes are now bounding into the nets with satisfying regularity. But none of these are vampires. Finally, at 8:00 p.m., Randy comes down from the summit to announce that he and Karen are snagging *Desmodus rotundus* in the lowest strands of the net placed over the vertical shaft. The vampire bats are coming up out of the adit and flowing over the lip of the shaft like morning mist. They have already captured four and another one has escaped. Needless to say, the report sends us all scurrying to the top of the mountain. Only Barry, more patient than the rest of us, remains to man the quieter nets below.

Success assured, we cluster around the vertical shaft and await developments. But the rush is already over. Few bats of any kind are coming out now. The talk turns to vampyres and other folklore as Ernesto and José Maria tell us about *duendes*, diminutive men who never show their faces and who inhabit such places as this. It is late August, inky black, and a colossal summer thunderstorm is raging over the Sierra de los Alamos to the east. As we watch the *relampágo* and listen to the *trueno*, José Maria cautions us that the storm may come this way as storms to the east almost always do. But later he seems to alter his opinion, hoping that the storm may go around us.

We are untangling another vampire bat from the net when a lightning bolt of awesome brilliance smashes into the ground next to a *palo santo* tree only a few meters away, capturing the gloomy hillside like a giant flash bulb. Within seconds, drops of rain come splattering down, and José Maria pronounces that it is time to *vamos*. But it is too late. Hardly are the words out of his mouth than the sky breaks open in a terrific downpour. Never have I felt rain like this. Sheets of water are pouring down my back, and the beam of my headlamps only penetrates a few feet. Instinctively I grab the pillowcase containing the vampire bats, and scramble down the mountain.

I would certainly lose my way if it were not for the constant flashes of lightning that come with the frequency of a light being turned on and off. Still, I can barely see, and can only sense the presence of Randy and Karen wrestling with the net and poles behind me. Yet, the constant drenching only increases in intensity. Fearful of falling into one of the many shafts, I drop down on all fours to make my way down the slippery slope. Finally, after an eternity has passed I feel rather than find my way along the path that leads to the trucks. But my relief is short-lived as dampness turns to pain. The rain has turned to hail and I seriously wonder if all of us can make it to the shelter before succumbing to the cold. Bending low, so as to protect our booty of vampire bats, I stumble onward.

But all is well. I can see the headlights of a truck and the next lightning flash reveals Ernesto and José Maria esconced under the eaves of an abandoned shed. Hollers and shrieks tell me that Randy and Karen are right behind me. Barry, bless his heart, is on the lea side of the hill, busy untangling a golden-red *Desmodus* from a net that was left up too long. At last I feel the truck door's handle. The downpour will last for nearly an hour. But I care not. Happiness is being cold and wet in a truck with a sack full of vampire bats.

Wanting to know more about our captive goblins (which we released the next evening), I have since consulted what can only be described as an extensive body of published works on these "little children of the night." Because the common vampire is an economic pest and a health threat in Latin America, several scientists have devoted their careers and a considerable part of their life to the study of this animal. Especially informative were *The Vampire Bat -- a presentation of undescribed habits and review of its history* by R.L. Ditmars and A.M. Greenhall, Walter Dalquest's *Natural History of the Vampire Bats of Eastern Mexico*, D.C. Turner's *The Vampire Bat -- a field study in behavior and ecology*, G. Clay Mitchell's *Vampire Bat Control in Latin America*, and most importantly, the comprehensive *Natural History of Vampire Bats* by Arthur M. Greenhall and Uwe Schmidt. What I found out from these and other publications was as fascinating as it was instructive. To communicate this knowledge is the purpose of this book. Hopefully, you will find this information as entertaining as I did.

David E. Brown

5

INTRODUCTION

> It must be like a Vision of Judgement to awake
> suddenly and to find on the tip of one's nose, in the act of
> drawing one's life blood, that demonical face with deformed
> nose, satyrlike ears, and staring saucer eyes, backed by a
> body measuring two feet from wing-end to wing-end.

> Sir Richard Francis Burton, 1869,
> *The Highlands of the Brazil*

Bats in a variety of guises have been much in the public eye of late. Batman, one of the comic book superheroes of the 1940s and 50s has recently graduated to the big screen, enjoying considerable box office success in the process. Vampyres, those immortal souls who rise from their graves to feed upon the blood of their living brethren, are featured in and out of bat form in a seemingly endless parade of novels, short-stories, television soap operas, tabloid newspapers, and cartoon comics. So popular are vampyre legends with modern audiences, that these nighttime ghouls were the subjects of no fewer than three major motion pictures in 1992, including yet another version of Bram Stoker's perennially favorite novel, *Dracula*. Real bats, too, are becoming increasingly popular in the media, thanks to a growing cadre of bat enthusiasts. Bat advocates even have their own political action groups, including Bat Conservation International, one of several organizations which seeks to inform the public that these uniquely flying mammals are both interesting and beneficial.

There are good and long-standing reasons for our fascination with bats and bat-like creatures, a phenomenon that precedes the written word and goes back to the time when we first grappled with the concepts of death, the human soul, and the possibility of a nether-world. Bats, being creatures of the night, have always been associated with mystery and the unknown, emerging as they do from caverns and other adits to the underworld. Their ability to fly bird-like on naked, membranous wings instills a sense of awe and envy, and their capacity to avoid obstacles in the dark gives them an almost supernatural aspect. As if these attributes were not mystical enough, their faces and bodies can, with a little imagination, take on an eerie resemblance to the human form. Female bats have paired breasts similar to a woman's, and like their human counterparts, usually only bear one young at a time. Bats not only have forward-looking eyes that give them human-like expressions, many species possess alert, fox-like ears and exaggerated sexual organs that are ready-made for myths and

7

superstitions. No wonder that so many of the gargoyles and fallen angels portrayed by medieval artists come with bat-like features.

Man's relationships with bats have ranged from all-out-war to mutually beneficial. Bats have been, and continue to be, eaten, worshipped, loathed, feared, persecuted, exploited, and praised. Bats in Samoa are managed as edible game; in other countries they are sought out and killed as destroyers of fruit or carriers of disease. Bats have also contributed to medical research and aided in the study of human diseases. Their echolocation techniques are similar to the SONAR used to detect enemy submarines. Millions of tons of bat guano were mined in the 1800s and made into fertilizer and gunpowder. During World War II, plans were made to equip thousands of bats with miniature incendiary bombs, in the hope that these reclusive animals would cause widespread infernos when released over Japanese cities. Even now, some people continue to destroy bats as household nuisances while others value them as insect controllers and even make pets of them.

Given our infringements on their lives, bats have proven themselves to be extraordinarily resilient. Despite massive habitat destruction and the widespread use of insecticides, less than a dozen species of bats are listed as "endangered" by U.S. Fish and Wildlife Service and the International Union for the Conservation of Nature. Only one species of bat, the Greater Mascarene flying fox of Mauritius and Reunion islands (home of the equally unfortunate dodo birds), is known to have become extinct in historic times, although another island species, the Guam flying fox, may now have also disappeared. The only New World bat deemed rare enough to be prohibited from trade by the Convention for International Trade in Endangered Species is the white-lined bat of Central America. Even among those bats which are classified as "endangered," the actual status of such species as the lesser long-nosed bat of the American Southwest and Mexico is a matter of hot debate among biologists.

Contrary to just a few years ago, bats are now getting some good press. And well they should. Not only are these flying mammals rightfully touted as natural destroyers of insect pests and pollinators of valued plants, they are rapidly gaining recognition for their unusual variations and adaptability. Indeed, one sometimes wonders how bats found enough roosting sites before we provided them with mine shafts, bridges, tunnels, and vacant buildings. And, just as we are now beginning to appreciate bats, we are learning that their ranks contain some of the most interesting and specialized animals on earth.

There are somewhere between 850 and 1000 kinds of bats. Nobody knows just how many. New species are yet being discovered, and mammalogists are reclassifying others. Some bats are known only from a single museum specimen. And, because animal taxonomy is not an exact science, there will always be disagreement as to which forms are species and which ones are only races or subspecies. Bats have been around for more than fifty million years and have had time to evolve into a myriad of shapes and sizes.

The largest living bat is the *Kalong*, a so-called "flying fox" of Indonesia, which can weigh up to two pounds and have a wingspan approaching six feet. By way of contrast, the recently discovered bumblebee bat of Thailand has only a six-inch wingspan and is the world's tiniest mammal, weighing in at a mere seven hundredths of an ounce or less than a penny! In the New World, the record for the biggest goes to the giant spear-nosed bat, a tropical predator which can boast a wing span of 3 1/3 feet and tip the scales at a hefty 2/5 of a pound. The smallest American bat, the diminutive western pipistrelle, has a wingspan of only about eight inches and weighs around 1/4 of an ounce.

Although most bats are brown or gray in color, some are real beauties. One of the brightest examples is the appropriately named "painted bat" of the Asian tropics with its brilliant fire-orange fur with black "patch-work" wings. There are red bats, black bats, yellow bats, and even white bats. Some species come with spotted pelage, others are striped, and a few are naked or nearly so. And, while the faces of some bats have been variously described as hideous, grotesque, and repulsive, others come across as decidedly handsome, and some are even cute and cuddly. There are bats with faces resembling bulldogs; others look like pigs, hares, foxes, cats, or mice. Still others have the features of Chihuahuas and other breeds of dogs. Another, the flower-faced bat, has a face to match its name.

Bats range from the Equator to the Arctic Circle and are found at elevations from sea-level to timberline. Those in cold climes escape the rigors of winter by migrating or hibernating; southern species go forth every night of the year to make a living. There are tropical forest bats, mountain-dwelling bats, grassland bats, and desert bats. Their daytime roost may be in a cave, a forgotten mineshaft, various parts of a tree, a bird's nest, or a secluded recess in your attic. At least one species, the tent-building bat, makes its own shelter by cutting the ribs of a leaf-frond and roosts under the hanging portion of the umbrella it has created. Some bats, like the Mexican free-tailed bat, roost in colonies with thousands and even millions of their kind; others seek a solitary existence or live in pairs.

More than just the habitats are apportioned out. All bats are more or less nocturnal, but certain times of the night are favored by some species over others. Most insect-feeders are out at first dusk in the early evening. Some fruit-eaters and meat-eaters prefer the darkest hours of the night. Other species feed by moonlight, or are active just before dawn. Many bats forage high above the tree tops, while others, like the desert-dwelling pallid bat, do their hunting close to, or even on, the ground. A few bats make their living in deep woods, others haunt forest openings, and still others seek their prey over water. Some flitter about like butterflies; others are strong and rapid flyers. The long-winged bat has been clocked at more than forty miles per hour -- a speed equivalent to a mourning dove or a fleeing pronghorn antelope.

Most bats eat insects, but a number of species subsist mainly on a variety of fruit. Species like the long-tongued bat are specialized to feed on flower pollen and nectar. A few catch and consume fish or shrimp, while some live on frogs. There are also bats that prey on birds, small rodents, and even other bats. The meat-eating false vampires and ghost bats of Asia, Africa, and Australia are even said to decapitate their victims before partaking of their flesh.

No bat, however, so fires our imagination and is more renowned than the common vampire bat of tropical America. The vampire's singular diet of warm blood, its stealthy nighttime attacks on man and his livestock, and its capability of transmitting deadly diseases -- all strike us with fear mixed with fascination. That the vampire bat prefers torrid climes and hostile jungles, adds to the animal's sinister reputation.

It should therefore come as no surprise that the vampire bat has assumed not only the real-life role, but acquired the persona of its mythical Old World counterpart. And, by giving this bat the ability to metamorphose in and out of human form in countless horror stories and films, we have bestowed on this small mammal a notoriety unmatched by any other animal on earth. Nature and mythology have combined to make the vampire bat our worst nightmare come true. Indeed, reality and superstition are now so intertwined, that I have used the archaic English spelling of *vampyre* throughout the book for the legendary Old World blood-drinker to differentiate the supernatural being from the real vampire bat.

There are several reasons for publishing a popular book on vampire bats at this time. Not the least of these is the enormous amount of information available on the bat itself. Because of its unique natural history, the vampire bat has long intrigued scientists. Not only is this mammal's diet of liquid blood highly unusual, the bat's ability to withdraw a meal without alarming its donor has piqued man's interest for nearly 500 years. As if these attributes were not incentive enough for study, the vampire bat is a serious economic pest and a carrier of a fatal disease. It is also one of the few mammals to regularly feed on people.

The result of all these attributes has been a plethora of investigations into the vampire bat's life history by a cadre of investigators such as William Beebe, Raymond L. Ditmars, Arthur M. Greenhall, Walter Dalquest, Bernardo Villa, Uwe Schmidt, Samuel B. Linhart, G. Clay Mitchell, Dennis C. Turner, William A. Wimsatt,

10

Rexford Lord, and Gerald Wilkinson. These and other vampire hunters have labored, not only in the jungles, pastures, and villages of Mexico, Central America, South America, and Trinidad, but in laboratories throughout the world. Because of their efforts, a great deal is now known about this elusive animal. Details of the vampire bat's life history, behavior, and physiology literally fill hundreds of pages in scientific journals. We now also know that these bats are as intelligent and adaptable as they are physically remarkable. No less impressive is the fact that the common vampire bat has expanded its range and numbers in the face of some of the most ingenious control programs ever devised. Clearly, the vampire bat is one of nature's most successful survivors.

Of equal interest is the long and continuing heritage of vampire bat folklore. Hundreds of years before the original movie version of *Dracula*, in which the Count assumes the form of a bat, vampire bats were featured in the Maya creation myth as supernatural beings in disguise. If anything, this portrayal of vampire bats as powerful denizens of the night has increased with time. Today, vampire bats and vampyre beliefs co-mingle in countless myths and legends, inspiring every communication medium from word-of-mouth tales to full-length novels and feature films. All of which makes for an unusual story, one that combines fact, fiction, and folklore in almost equal proportions. Vampyres and vampire bats not only intrigue us, stories about them can be great fun.

PART I NATURAL HISTORY OF VAMPIRE BATS

> And in many places [there are] bats of such bigness,
> that they are equal with turtle doves. These bats, have often
> times assaulted men in the night in their sleep, and so bitten
> them with their venomous teeth, that they have been thereby
> almost driven to madness, in so much that they have been
> compelled to flee from such places, as from ravenous harpies.

> Pietro Martyre Anghiera, 1510
> Transcribed from an Old English
> translation by Richard Eden.

DISCOVERY BY SCIENCE

Stories of blood-sucking bats began circulating in Europe
shortly after Columbus returned from his third voyage to Trinidad and
the coast of South America in 1498. But sailors also told fanciful tales
of giants, sea monsters, and tribes of female warriors. Why not also
bats that sucked one's blood? The belief was that if you could imagine
some creature, it probably existed somewhere in the new lands that
were then being discovered yearly.

But, unlike many sea-stories, the tales of blood-drinking bats
persisted. Letters describing men and their animals being assaulted by
these "winged leeches" followed in the wake of the *conquistadores*, and
as early as 1526 a Castilian soldier-of-fortune turned historian named
Gonzalo Fernando de Oviedo provided a reasonably accurate
description of the bats and their blood-letting abilities:

> ". . . these bats are neither more nor less than those
> here, and are accustomed to bite at night, and commonly bite
> mostly on the end of the nose or the fleshy part of the fingers
> or toes. They take so much blood that it is something that
> can't be believed without seeing..."

Francisco de Montejo complained of bats bleeding his horses
and troops during his conquest of Yucatán in 1527, and in 1565
Girolame Benzoni grumbled about the numbers of "tormenting bats"
infesting the Caribbean coast between Costa Rica and Trinidad. Like
Oviedo in Panama, Benzoni spoke from first-hand knowledge, the bats
having "pecked my toes so delicately that I did not feel it at all; yet in
the morning I found the sheets and mattresses so stained with blood,
that it seemed as if they had inflicted some great injury."

13

But the explorers who first penetrated the New World tropics, while astute observers of local conditions, were primarily interested in gold, slaves, and souls, not in natural history. Furthermore, any information obtained about the wonders of "Earthly Paradise" was jealously secreted in the archives of Spain and Portugal lest other European powers somehow benefit from the hard-won knowledge of their conquistadors and colonists. Except for the literal pirating of Spanish correspondence, and the copying of Spanish and Portuguese documents by well-placed spies, the natural history of Latin America remained a mystery to the rest of Europe for nigh on 250 years.

It was not until the middle of the 18th Century, beginning with the expedition of Charles-Marie de LaCondimine and his colleagues in the French Royal Academy, that outside scientists were finally allowed a peek at Central and South America's natural treasures. Once opened, however, Latin America proved to be an irresistible draw to Europe's naturalists. Its jungles, swamps, and savannas were soon to be penetrated by a new breed of conquistador who collected examples of anything that grew or moved. For the next 200 years botanists and animal collectors roamed the countryside, not looking for gold or silver, but in search of specimens for the burgeoning museums of Europe, and later, the United States. Moreover, reports of blood-drinking bats would now be subjected to the scrutiny of scientific investigation.

Almost every early naturalist-explorer -- de LaCondimine, Alexander von Humboldt, Alfred Russel Wallace, Henry Walter Bates, and Charles Darwin, to name only a few -- witnessed the work of "blood-sucking bats" during their travels. The problem was that the bats always came at night while the observer was asleep, and no one was quite certain as to just which bat or bats were the blood-letters. Even the Indians were vague on this point, and it was commonly assumed that the nose-leaf or "spear" on the nose of certain bats somehow functioned as a device to open wounds and accommodate the animal's blood-drinking propensities. Accordingly, various species of bats, especially the larger, more "hideous looking" ones, were thought to be the culprits. Oftentimes the naturalists were no better than the laymen when it came to powers of observation, and a number of bats, not only from South America but also from the Far East, were mistakenly thought to subsist on the blood of living humans and animals. Hence, many species were given scientific names that reflected European legends of blood-sucking vampyres and spectres -- *Vampyrops*, *Vampyrodes*, and *Vampyressa*. With a wingspan exceeding three feet, the giant spear-nosed or spectral vampire bat, named *Vampyrum spectrum* by Linnaeus in 1758, was widely, but erroneously believed to be *the* principal blood-letting bat throughout South and Central America until well into the 1800s.

Figure 1. Early drawing of *Vampyrum spectrum* (Giant Spearnosed Bat). This species was once thought to be the principal blood-drinking bat of South and Central America.

That at least one of the "blood-suckers" was a small bat was known as early as 1769, and in 1801 a Spanish cartographer turned naturalist named Felix de Azara, identified the bat we now recognize as the common vampire bat as the one most often biting humans and animals. But even though this bat became locally known in parts of Paraguay as *mordedor de Azara* (Azara's biter), most naturalists were still ignorant of which bat, or bats, were the ones plaguing man and his livestock. French and German zoologists, who had acquired specimens of the same bat as de Azara had, failed to recognize its unique adaptations to feeding on blood, and made no mention of its blood-drinking behavior in their scientific descriptions of the animal.

It was not until 1832, when Charles Darwin and his servant witnessed a bat drawing blood from a horse and collected the proven offender, that the English-speaking world began to accept blood-feeding bats as a scientific fact. Darwin's "vampire bat" was the same species as the bat collected by de Azara 30 years earlier in Paraguay, and which had first been described by zoologists in 1810. After a confusing sequence of scientific names, the animal, which we now call the common vampire bat, was eventually given the Latin name of *Desmodus rotundus*. Nonetheless, despite the observations of Darwin and other eminent biologists, some naturalists still thought that blood-feeding bats were the product of an over-active imagination. Others continued to believe that the real "blood-sucker" was the huge spectral vampire bat, and still others held to the opinion that several species of

15

bats fed on blood. Even as late as the 1880s, it was still generally agreed upon that at least two species of vampire bats existed, a large two foot model that fed on horses and cows, and a smaller one that preyed on fowls. That the diminutive *Desmodus* was the source of 400 years of bloodthirsty bat stories was not generally appreciated until the 19th Century was nearly at a close.

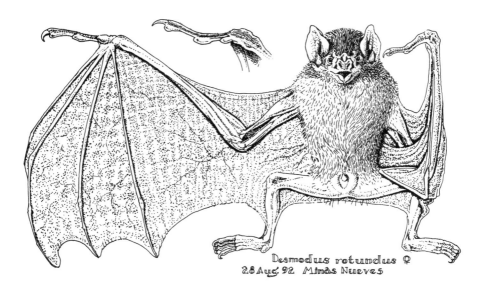

Figure 2. Common Vampire Bat (*Desmodus rotundus*). Note the elongated thumb, lack of a tail, and absence of a noseleaf. Drawn from life by Randy Babb.

Those that contended that several species of bat dined on blood were not entirely in error, however. Another small bat, first described in 1823 from a specimen collected in Brazil, was later shown to also be a true vampire in that it feeds entirely on fresh blood. Relatively uncommon, this bat, called the hairy-legged vampire bat (*Diphylla ecaudata*) preys largely on birds. An even rarer vampire bat -- the white-winged vampire, *Diaemus youngi*, was not discovered until 1893 when one was collected in what is now Guyana. Given the vampire bat's long notoriety as a blood-letter, and the large number of bats described as vampires, it is somewhat ironic that zoologists described two of the three species of true vampire bats *before* knowing of their sanguinary habits.

Figure 3. Hairy-legged Vampire Bat (*Diphylla ecaudata*). Among other differences, this generally furrier bat has a shorter thumb and rounder ears than the common vampire bat. Drawn from a preserved specimen by Randy Babb.

Figure 4. White-winged Vampire Bat (*Diaemus youngi*). Note the white wing tips and white fourth (index) finger. Drawn from a study skin by Randy Babb.

17

The scientific name of the common vampire, *Desmodus rotundus* literally means "fused-toothed and round" (*Desmos* = bundled or fused together; *odus* from the Greek *odontos* or tooth; and *rotundus*, Latin meaning rotund or spherical in shape). These names refer to the fact that the bat's huge upper incisors and canine teeth are so large that they appear to be joined at their bases, and the rounded shape of the skull's dome-like cranium. The bat's rotund body, especially when engorged with blood, also makes the common vampire's scientific name appropriate.

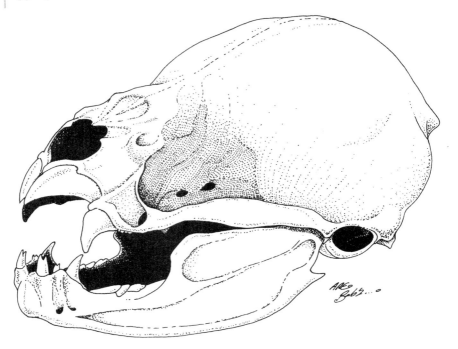

Figure 5. Skull of a common vampire bat. No other bat has so prominent a pair of upper incisors. Drawing by Randy Babb.

COMMON NAMES

This is the Bat to which Linnaeus applied the title of Vampyre, on the supposition of its being the species of which so many extraordinary accounts have been given relative to its power of sucking the blood both of men and cattle.

George Shaw, *General Zoology*, 1800

Even in Darwin's day, those bats thought to be "blood-suckers" were popularly referred to as vampires in English, or in Spanish, *vampiros*. Few animals are more suitably named. "Vampire" or "Vampyre" is a Slavonic word meaning "blood drunkenness" and is the name given to the mythological living dead whose corpses rise from their graves at night to feed on the blood of sleeping persons. In the late 1600s an epidemic of vampyre hysteria began in eastern Europe that continued at intermittent intervals until reaching a crescendo in the early 1730s. These tales of blood-drinking ghouls spread throughout the continent, firing the imaginations of the peasants and intelligentsia alike. It was only natural then that by the 1750s the term "vampyre" (= "vampire") was being applied to reputed blood-feeding bats, not only those from the New World, but to bats in Asia, Africa, and Australia as well. So pervasive were stories of "blood-sucking" bats that even some of the little European species were falsely accused of the practice. By the mid-1800s the vampyre or vampire appellation for "blood-drinking" bats was in general usage, hence popularizing both the bat's name and the vampyre legend. That a real animal could have so many characteristics in common with imaginary blood-drinking spectres has resulted in many people thinking that the vampyre myth gets its name from the bat. No so. It is just the opposite.

When one speaks of vampire bats he or she is almost always referring to the common vampire bat. The term "common vampire bat" is usually only used by biologists to differentiate this bat from the lesser known hairy-legged and white-winged vampire bats. Because hairy-legged and white-winged vampires are so uncommon, the descriptions and discussions of vampire bats in this book apply to the common vampire unless stated otherwise.

Vampire bats in Spanish-speaking America are properly called *murciélagos vampiros* (vampire bats) or *murciélagos hematofagos* (blood-feeding bats). Besides being commonly referred to simply as *vampiros* or *vampiros de sangria*, vampire bats in parts of Mexico and Central America are also appropriately known as *mordedores* (biters) or *sanguesugas* (blood-suckers). In Portuguese-speaking Brazil, vampire bats are called *morcegos hamatophagos* or "blood-feeding bats." So powerful is the vampire's reputation relative to other bats, that many rural people in vampire bat country consider all or most species of bats to be *vampiros*. Those asking local people as to the presence or whereabouts of vampire bats had best beware.

DESCRIPTION

> VAMPYRE BAT -- Of this tremendous animal there
> are some varieties in point of size and colour; or perhaps they
> may really be distinct races or species, though nearly allied.
> The largest or the Great Ternate Bat, is, in general, about a
> foot long, with an extent of wings about four feet; but
> sometimes it is found far larger, and it has been said that
> specimens have been seen of six feet in extent.
>
> George Shaw, *General Zoology*, 1800

General Appearance: Almost everyone has heard of vampire
bats but relatively few people have ever seen one. Even in the
countries where it is found, the animal is strictly nocturnal and avoids
both natural and artificial light. Should one be captured, moreover, the
creature appears at first glance to be just another medium-sized bat.
Yet, even the most cursory examination soon shows it to be special.
Unlike other bats, this "little hellion" shrieks in fury at being handled,
and fights back with surprising strength and dexterity. At rest, the
mouth is formed in such a manner that the bat appears to disquietly
grin at its captor. Any sudden movement or sound results in a
remarkably swift response. Its spherical body, while small, is compact
and muscular. When baring its prominent incisors, this "miniature
gargoyle" displays a set of surgical-sharp fangs which are guaranteed to
pierce the flesh of all but the most wary. The tongue is long, pointed,
and pink in color.

Figure 6. Close-up view of the facial features of a common vampire bat.
Photo by Randy Babb.

Figure 7. "Split" lower lip of a vampire bat. Photo by Randy Babb.

Further scrutiny reveals the bat to have a short neck and a pug nose, giving its face a bull-dog appearance. No prominent nose-leaf or "spear" is present, but a small nose-pad rises above a U-shaped fold on the bat's abbreviated snout. The vampire bat has no tail whatsoever. Only a narrow membrane, called a *uropatagium*, connects the vampire's long hind legs with its rump. Its dark-colored eyes are surprisingly large for a bat that spends its life in darkness. Set low on the face, they peer inquisitively forward, and watchfully follow every move. The ears, though generous, are not especially large for a bat, and their slightly pointed tips contribute to the vampire's diabolical expression. The *tragus*, the earlet or flap above the notch of the finely-ribbed ear that is assumed to assist bats in echolocation, is triangular in shape and mostly hairless. A deep fold on the jutting lower lip accentuates the slightly gaping mouth and gives the impression that the bat has a split lip. The sex organs, especially the male's, are conspicuous.

The bat's pelage is short and fine as befits an animal living in a warm climate, although individual hairs vary enough in length to give the bat a rather unkempt appearance when compared to most tropical bats. The legs and other extremities are even more thinly furred, and the bat's back is noticeably darker than its underparts. The wings are naked and look like fine leather. Most vampire bats are varied shades of gray above and silvery gray underneath. In some individuals the

21

drab gray may be replaced by a dull brown. There is also a henna color phase, and some vampire bats have even been reported to be bright orange. A captive albino, pink eyes and all, was featured in the October 16, 1937, issue of the *Illustrated London News*, and one we caught near Alamos in Sonora, Mexico, was a beautiful golden color.

Figure 8. Elongated "thumb" of a common vampire bat. Photo by Randy Babb.

The vampire bat's most diagnostic features, however, are its elongated thumbs and its specialized teeth. Indeed, the 2/3 to 3/4 inch-long "thumb" on the leading edge of the wing is longer than the bat's entire hind foot. With its three sole-like pads, this appendage is long enough and strong enough to serve as a front foot, thus allowing the vampire to silently run about on all fours.

The skull of a vampire bat has a highly domed cranium and two projecting, massive front incisors that quickly distinguish it from all other bats. The sharply pointed and scoop-like upper incisors are joined at their bases by equally impressive canines, the cutting edges of the two teeth forming a 'V'-like gap. These teeth have no enamel and are reported to be self-sharpening by a process called *thegosis* in which the upper teeth come in contact with the lower incisors every time the mouth is closed. Both the upper incisors and canines are incredibly sharp, and people have been "bitten" just by handling the skull of a vampire. On the lower jaw, only the canines are pointed and sharp; the small peg-like front teeth have cusps designed to grasp the skin of an intended victim, and are widely spaced to permit a protruding tongue to lap its blood. As would be expected of an animal restricted to a liquid diet, the molars are small and without grinding surfaces. With only 20 teeth in its head, the vampire has fewer teeth, not more, than other bats.

Figure 9. Common vampire bat with open mouth showing upper incisors. Photo by Randy Babb.

Lengths and Weights: Vampires are not large bats as is commonly portrayed, their bodies being about the size of a house mouse. The wing span of full-size adults is only between 13 and 14 inches. Females tend to be larger and heavier than the males, and fully grown vampire bats will range in length from about 2 3/4 inches to 3 1/2 inches from the tip of the nose to the end of their rump. Weights can vary from as little as one ounce to 1 3/4 ounces for a well-fed individual. Vampires in some areas tend to be heavier than in others, and those from Paraguay and other regions near the Tropic of Capricorn are reported to be larger than those farther north.

Spoor: Almost as soon as a cave or other retreat used by large numbers of vampire bats is entered, one detects a strong stench of ammonia that is distinctly different than the normal odor of bat guano. The bats typically form a tight cluster of from half a dozen to several hundred individuals on the cave's ceiling, and a deposit of black liquid feces collects under these roosts. These stinking, tar-like pools of digested blood are unmistakable, and a sure sign that vampire bats are present. As if the stench and oil-like consistency of these decaying pools of goop were not disgusting enough, cockroaches, huge spiders, and other scavengers scurry about the edge of the drying mass. The mess itself often contains the remains of dying and deceased bats. Vampire bats periodically change the location of their roosts, and the relative shininess as well as the viscosity of the deposits can be used to determine which sites are currently occupied. A dull smear of dried black stains indicates a temporary roost which is no longer in use.

Normal vampire bat droppings are never red or scarlet colored as some might suppose. Reddish-colored droppings in a cave or mineshaft are the dietary results of the presence of one or more species of fruit-eating bats.

Other Vampire Bats: Both the hairy-legged and white-winged vampire bats are similar in size to the common vampire bat. As its name implies, the hairy-legged vampire bat can be differentiated from its more common cousin by the presence of fur along the inner side of its rear legs and on the fringes of the uropatagium. These areas are naked, or nearly so, on the common vampire bat. The hairy-legged vampire also lacks any pads on the underside of its shorter thumbs, and its lower incisor teeth are fan-shaped and oddly lobed. Compared to the common vampire, the hairy-legged vampire's brownish fur is longer and finer. These animals are also uniformly colored above and below, and the ears are more rounded. Hairy-legged vampire bats are slightly smaller than their common vampire cousins, adults ranging from 2 1/2 to 3 1/2 inches in length and averaging little more than an ounce in weight. Unlike the black tar-like pools left by the common vampire bat, the hairy-legged vampire's droppings are rusty brown smears or stains.

Figure 10. Hairy-legged vampire bat. Note hairy rear legs and short "thumb." U.S. Fish & Wildlife Service photo courtesy of Clay Mitchell.

The even rarer white-winged vampire is a reddish brown in color and has pure white wing tips along with a white index finger on the leading edge of each wing. Its feet also lack pads, and its thumbs are similar to the hairy-legged's. Weighing a little more than an ounce, this small bat is about 3 1/3 inches in length. The white-winged vampire bat's eyes are large and shiny black, and its eyelids appear noticeably thick. When agitated, the bat emits a nauseous, skunk-like odor accompanied by a spitting hiss from two large cup-shaped glands in the rear of its mouth. This bat, like its more common relative, also excretes black, tar-like feces.

Figure 11. Fruit bat of the genus *Artibeus*. These small bats are commonly mistaken for vampire bats. Although the two bats are about the same size and color, the fruit bat has a large leaf-like appendage on its nose, lacks prominent upper incisors, and possesses faint face stripes. Photo by Randy Babb.

False Vampire Bats

Ijurra shot a large bat, of the vampire species, measuring about two feet across the extended wings. This is a very disgusting looking animal, though its fur is very delicate, and of a glossy, rich maroon color. Its mouth is amply provided with teeth, looking like that of a miniature tiger... The nostrils seem fitted as a suction apparatus. Above them is a triangular, cartilaginous snout, nearly half an inch long, and a quarter broad at the base; and below them is a semi-circular flap, of nearly the same breadth, but not so long. I suppose these might be placed over the puncture made by the teeth, and the air underneath exhausted by the nostrils, thus making them a very perfect cupping-glass.

> Lieutenant William Lewis Herndon, U.S. Navy, *Exploration of the Valley of the Amazon*, 1854

As their Latin names imply, several species of bats were once thought to be "vampires" on the basis of their ferocious appearance, or through an erroneous interpretation of their feeding habits. So ingrained was the reputation of some of these bats, that they are commonly called "false vampires." This is especially so of two species of large leaf-nosed bats from Central and South America, Linneaus' false vampire (*Vampyrum spectrum*) and the spear-nosed or javelin bat (*Phyllostomus hastatus*). These bats, while not feeding on blood, are nonetheless predatory meat-eaters, attacking and feeding on a variety of bats as well as on other small animals.

Equally worthy of the "false vampire" appellation are several species of carnivorous Old World bats. Despite being only distantly related to the false vampires of the Americas, these bats are also tailless (or nearly so), possess erect nose-leaves, and feed on small mammals including other bats. The giant false vampires and ghost bats of Asia and Australia are especially impressive looking predators. One of these, the Australian or Indian false vampire bat was once called the "great blood-sucking bat" because it had supposedly been seen sucking the blood of a smaller bat. In truth, this species, *Megaderma lyra*, has been reported to first decapitate a victim and drink its blood before devouring their flesh! None of these so-called false vampire bats subsists entirely on blood, however, and "true" vampire bats are only found in the New World.

FOSSIL HISTORY

> While any positive virtue of the vampire in nature's scheme have thus far eluded us, the animal does challenge the interest of the biologist, who sees in its specialized diet and habits fascinating problems in comparative anatomy, physiology and behavior, evolution and public health.

> William A. Wimsatt, *Portrait of a Vampire*, 1959

Bones of vampire bats have been recovered from about 20 fossil deposits, all of them in caves or natural fissures in North or South

America. None of these sites has been dated at more than two million years old, and most are less than 35,000 years old. Although sounding ancient, these ages are relatively recent in evolutionary time, and except for size, all of the fossil vampire bats are similar to those living today. And, despite such names as *Provampyrus* having been applied to extinct Old World bats, no fossil of a true vampire bat has ever been found in the Eastern Hemisphere.

Vampire bats represented by fossils include both the existing common and hairy-legged vampires as well as three extinct species -- *Desmodus archaeodaptes*, *Desmodus stocki*, and the wonderfully named *Desmodus draculae*. *Desmodus archaeodaptes*, the oldest known vampire bat, has been recovered from two locations in Florida where it may have lived as long as 1.5 million years ago. *Desmodus stocki*, or Stock's vampire bat, has been found from California and West Virginia south into Mexico. Stock's vampire bat, while closely related to the modern vampire bat, was about 20% larger than its modern cousin. This northern species was found with giant ground sloths and other recently extinct large mammals, and Stock's vampire bat may have been present when humans first arrived in the Americas around 10,000 years ago.

Figure 12. Prehistoric vampire bats feeding on a giant ground sloth. Drawing by Randy Babb.

Even larger, with a wing-span of over two feet, was *Desmodus draculae*, recovered from fossil deposits in Venezuela's Cuevo del Guacharo, the caverns where Alexander von Humbolt found the *guacharo* or oil bird. These deposits, and another site in Yucatán yielding a fossil vampire bat similar in size to *Desmodus draculae*, contain the bones of modern day animals, including the still existing common and hairy-legged vampires bats. It is therefore not beyond the realm of possibility that this largest of all vampire bats still lives, remaining to be discovered in some as yet unexplored region of the Amazon Basin! What such a large vampire would feed upon would of course present a problem -- tapirs, perhaps.

These fossils are also of interest in that they show that vampire bats were formerly present in areas where they no longer occur. The 6,000 to 35,000 year-old remains of Stock's vampire bats in California and the Channel Islands, southwestern New Mexico, and west Texas, suggests that these areas had a more moderate climate then than now. It may be that vampire bats were eliminated from what is now the United States by the increasingly variable climate that accompanied the end of the last Ice Age between 7,000 and 12,000 years ago. Also, the mass extinction during this time of many large North American mammals, such as the giant ground sloth, may have denied blood-feeding bats an important source of food, causing vampire bats to become extinct in Cuba and southern Florida.

Because the fossil record is scanty and confined to relatively recent times, the origins of today's vampire bats are difficult to ascertain. On the basis of body structure and other criteria, scientists have determined that all vampire bats belong to the Phyllostomidae, a family of New World leaf-nosed bats that also contains carnivorous species as well as insect-eaters, nectar-feeders, and fruit-eaters. One hypothesis is that some leaf-nosed bat ancestor adapted itself to feeding on insects attracted to the wounds found in large herds of grazing mammals. Gradually, sometime between two and 10 million-years-ago, these bats took to feeding on blood flowing from the wounds themselves. Others believe that the vampire bat's ancestors were nectar-feeders. Just how this bizarre method of feeding came about is just one of the vampire bat's many secrets.

RANGE AND DISTRIBUTION

Nothing now prevents these creatures from migrating into Texas or other Southwestern states, to prey on huge herds of livestock.

Arthur H. Greenhall, "Profile of a Vampire," 1952

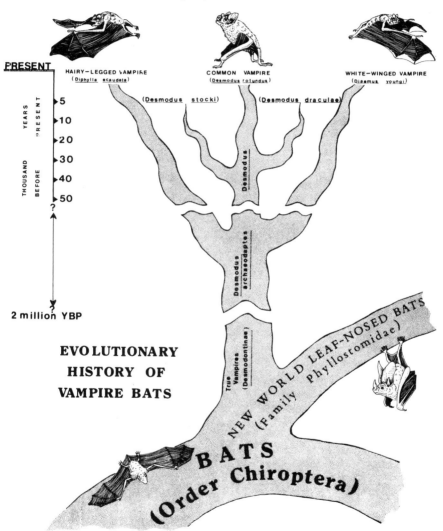

Figure 13. Evolutionary history of vampire bats. Drawing by Randy Babb.

All three species of vampire bats are neotropical animals. The widely distributed common vampire bat is found throughout tropical Mexico, Central America, and South America to as far south as central Chile, northern Argentina and Uruguay. It has been found at altitudes ranging from sea level to as high as 10,000 feet near the equator in the mountains of Columbia and Peru. Vampire bats are absent from the high Andes, the high plateau of central Mexico, and the Baja California peninsula. Because of a lack of native prey, and their inability to fly long distances, vampire bats are also absent from Cuba, Puerto Rico, and other Caribbean islands with the exception of Trinidad and Margarita which are close to mainland South America.

Figure 14. Range of the common vampire bat. Drawing by Randy Babb.

Figure 15. Distribution of the hairy-legged vampire bat. Drawing by Randy Babb.

Figure 16. Distribution of the white-winged vampire bat. Drawing by Randy Babb.

Unlike the common vampire bat, which has greatly expanded its distribution and numbers since the introduction of domestic livestock, the relatively rare hairy-legged and white-winged vampires have more restricted ranges. In Mexico, these two bats are restricted to the east side of the Central Plateau where they range from southern Tamaulipas south to the Isthmus of Tehuantepec. Both species are also unreported from large areas of South America, and neither of these bats has been found west of the Andes Mountains. As is the case with the common vampire bat, the only populations of white-winged vampire bats in the Caribbean islands are found on Trinidad and Margarita. Moreover, there is good evidence that both of these species have been present on the island of Margarita only since the 1960s.

Northern Limits: Although the first record in a scientific journal of a vampire bat in the Mexican state of Sonora was not published until 1963, a Jesuit friar, Ignaz Pferfferkorn, had reported "blood-letting" bats pestering people and livestock in the southern portions of Sonora in the mid-1700s. Vampire bats have been known to be present in the subtropical deciduous forests around Alamos, Sonora, since at least the early 1950s, and this species is now locally common there. In 1957, Mexico's leading bat expert, Dr. Bernardo Villa, reported finding the desiccated remains of one of these bats near Potam, Sonora, at the southern edge of the Sonoran Desert. Since then, vampire bats and their bites on livestock have been noted with some regularity from the vicinity of San Bernardo 260 miles south of the Arizona line. In 1992, Mexican officials of the Alamos Municipal District's livestock grower's association reported a vampire bat captured near the town of Yecora, Sonora, a pine-oak woodland locale within 200 miles of the U.S. border. Whether these reports are indicative of a northern range expansion or are only the result of these bats now receiving more attention than formerly is difficult to say.

Records of vampire bats in eastern Mexico have also been creeping northward. In 1963, biologist Ticul Alvarez reported finding vampire bats in a cave near Rancho Santa Rosa and near the town of Jimenez in Tamaulipas. These collections advanced the northernmost locations for vampires in the state to within 120 miles of the Texas border. Dr. Villa, in his 1966 book, *Murciélagos de México*, shows a record of a common vampire bat collected in the state of Nuevo Leon only about 80 miles from the Texas border. Such accounts prompted a fear that the bat's arrival in Texas' cattle country were just a matter of time -- apprehensions that appeared to have been realized in 1967. On May 24 of that year, a man named E.E. Remington shot into a cluster of bats hanging from the ceiling of an abandoned railroad tunnel 12 miles west of Comstock in Val Verde County, Texas. One of the bats brought down was identified by biologists as a female hairy-legged vampire. This singular record from the Chihuahuan Desert, besides extending the known occurrence of this species northward by nearly 450 miles, is the first, and as yet only record of a vampire bat in the United States in modern times.

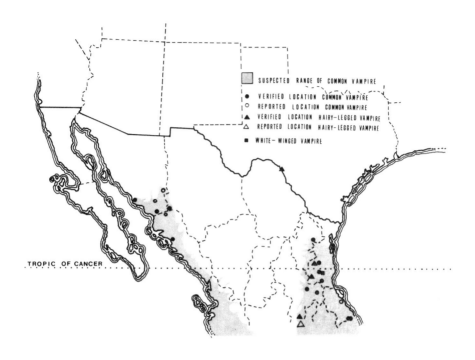

Figure 17. Northern distribution of vampire bats. Drawing by Randy Babb.

Additional investigations in Sonora and northeastern Mexico will likely lead to vampire bats being found even closer to the United States. This seemingly northward progression does not necessarily mean that the vampire bat is about to follow the example of the coatimundi and other tropical animals in taking up American citizenship, however. Biologists have noted that vampire bats are restricted to areas where the coldest month's average temperature remains above 50 degrees Fahrenheit. Because of the inability of vampire bats to cope with cold weather, and their need to feed nearly every night, an invasion of vampire bats into the American Southwest where freezing temperatures occur nearly every winter appears unlikely. Vampire bats neither hibernate nor migrate.

The vampire bat's apparent difficulty in maintaining sufficient body moisture in arid country also presents a problem. These bats have failed to take up permanent residence in either the Sonoran or Chihuahuan deserts despite the presence of livestock in these areas for centuries. Vampire bats might, however, become established in southern Florida, Cuba, or even the lower Rio Grande Valley. Like Africanized "killer" bees, any northward movement of vampire bats bears watching!

Habitat

Independent of the hollow trees, the Vampires have another hiding-place. They clear out the inside of the large ants' nests, and then take possession of the shell.

Charles Waterton, *Wanderings in South America*, 1825

Figure 18. Tropical semi-evergreen forest inhabited by vampire bats in Nayarit, Mexico. Photo by author.

Except for climatic limitations, vampire bats are not especially choosy about their outside surroundings, and range from coastal desert through tropical deciduous forests to evergreen rainforests. If winter temperatures are not too cold, the bat can even be found in pine-oak woods, cloud forests, and other temperate habitats. Nor is the bat a wilderness animal. Several investigators have commented that they found vampire bats to be more common in disturbed environments than in virgin forests -- an observation no doubt influenced by the bats' preference for livestock blood.

Figure 19. Abandoned mine occupied by vampire bats near Minas Nuevas, Sonora, Mexico. Photo by author.

Of more importance to the bat than the type of vegetation present is the availability of a suitable roost site in a humid cave, a forgotten mineshaft, or even an abandoned well or building. In drier and colder locales, subterranean roosts are particularly desirable because of their ameliorating surroundings. Such daytime refuges serve to provide the vampire's needs for both seclusion and compatible temperatures. Should a suitable cave or mine be lacking, vampire bats may roost in a hollow tree, and these bats have even been known to seek daytime retreats in rock crevices. On the Yucatán's limestone plateau, sinkholes called *cenotes*, provide ideal retreats. Suitable roost sites, along with a reliable supply of host animals, are the principal factors determining how many vampire bats may be found in a given area.

Figure 20. Hollow fig tree within tropical deciduous forest in Yucatán, Mexico. Photo by author.

Figure 21. Cenote used by vampire bats in Yucatán, Mexico. Photo by author.

PHYSICAL ABILITIES

While other species of bats sometimes slither along a ledge, they do so with their bodies flat against the rock, and they pull themselves along with tiny thumbs, which project from the elbow-like wrist joint.

Not so the vampires. They stood high on all fours -- on their long hind legs and their tremendous thumbs. No wonder they could dodge about so fast, even bounce around like rubber balls. They looked like some strange race of little men as they peered out at us.

Charles E. Mohr, "Cave of the Vampires," 1955

Agility on the Ground: The common vampire is the most agile of bats in that it not only flies well, it can climb vertical walls, and scuttle about on the ground with tightly folded wings. When necessary, it can even jump like a toad. No other bat is so well adapted to getting around on land. These wonderful means of locomotion are due to the bat's great upper body strength, its powerful forearms, and, most of all, to its specialized thumbs that act like front feet.

Figure 22. Vampire bat "running" along the wall of a cavern. Photo by Randy Babb.

As the bat scrambles crab-like over the surface, it need never turn its back on a foe. It can also immediately change course by hopping in whatever direction it desires. With a little extra effort, the jump becomes a leap, each bound carrying the bat six inches off the ground and covering a distance of a foot or more. Depending on its needs, the vampire can just as easily slow its gait to a stealthy stalk, or break into a bouncing run that propels the little hobgoblin forward at nearly five miles per hour -- a speed requiring a human pursuer to run to keep up. As if these characteristics were not un-batlike enough, vampire bats typically assume a "heads-up" posture when disturbed, their bodies inclined upward, held above the ground on their hind feet and the base of their thumbs, ready to spring into action. When so poised, they assume a posture not unlike an alert bear, wolf or other mammalian predator.

Flight: Vampire bats are wary animals, and are quick to flush when approached. Whether on the ground, or clinging upside down in its roost, the vampire springs into flight with a jump. If taking off from an elevated perch, the vampire sets its wings before taking flight rather than flapping its way airborne like other bats. If vampire bats are disturbed in a cave or other enclosed place, their wing beats make a peculiar swishing sound as they pass overhead that once heard is easily recognized. When traveling, however, the vampire's flight is silent and direct, the bat following selected flyways through the vegetation and along streamways. Vampires are also "daisy-cutters," usually flying only about three to six feet above the ground and rarely attaining an altitude much higher than ten feet. Flight is strong rather than swift, and although the vampire's maximum airspeed is unknown, their cruising speed has been estimated to only range between six and twelve miles per hour. And, while flashlight beams and other lights are adroitly avoided, vampires have little need to engage in the aerial acrobatics of their insect-catching kin.

Figure 23. Rio Corobici on Hacienda La Pacifica, Guanacaste Province, Costa Rica. Such streams are commonly used as "flyways" by vampire bats on their nightly rounds through the forest. Photo by the author.

Hearing and Echolocation: When it comes to earning a living, no sense is more important to the vampire bat than its remarkable hearing. This sense is so well developed that the bat can not only detect the sound of moving animals, it can hear them breathe. In contrast to many other bats, vampires hear low frequency ranges almost as well as they do ultrasonic sounds. This ability may not only help the bats locate their prey, it enables them to communicate through a variety of social calls. The vampire's vocal repertoire is therefore large, and excited or squabbling individuals frequently scream and shriek at each other at a frequency easily heard by humans. Softer, but still audible to humans, are the noises passed between grooming bats and by mothers and their young. The white-winged vampire bat is said to be even more vocal, emitting a variety of screams, chirps, whistles, and hisses.

Like most bats, vampires navigate by echolocation, that is by emitting high frequency sounds and responding to the echos of these sounds as they bounce back from obstacles. SONAR locates submarines in the same manner. Vampires are sometimes called "whispering" bats in that the echolocation calls sent through their open mouths are of comparatively low frequency and can be heard by people with a high hearing range. These calls are also emitted at a relatively constant frequency that is well suited for locating large objects. As a result, the vampire's ability to avoid fine obstacles such as nets and thin wires can only be rated as fair when compared to the echolocation abilities of insect-catching bats.

Eyesight and Sense of Smell: As their relatively large eyes suggest, vampires are not "blind as a bat," and have surprisingly good vision for an animal that spends its life in darkness. Their eyesight is reported to be comparable to that of a rat's, and vampires probably orient themselves visually as well as by echolocation when traveling. Besides responding to various shades of black, vampire bats have demonstrated an ability to recognize certain objects and patterns. As with most nocturnal animals, these bats are unable to detect the color red. Taking advantage of this limitation, biologist Arthur Greenhall used both red light and infra-red light in conjunction with military "snooper-scopes" to observe these bats on their nightly activities. Vampire bats can, however, discriminate between light and dark colors, and are said to select dark-colored cattle to feed on over lighter colored animals. Vision is nonetheless not as important for navigation and prey selection as hearing or smell.

Vampire bats have a well developed sense of smell and may be able to find their prey on the basis of odor alone. The vampire's sense of smell may also be used to select an individual prey animal, and could explain the well known fact that vampires repeatedly attack certain victims while ignoring others in the same building or pasture -- perhaps some individuals smell "better" than others. Some biologists are also of the opinion that vampire bats select cows in heat more than other cattle. The "smell of blood" does not attract vampire bats, however. In an experiment conducted by Dennis Turner in Costa Rica, vampire bats showed no preference for cattle swabbed with blood over those doused with water. Odor is also used to recognize roostmates, even though the vampire's scent glands are not particularly well developed. Every interaction between vampires begins with one or both bats intensely sniffing the other.

Special heat-sensing pits surrounding the vampire's nose pad allow the bat to detect the slightest difference in temperature. This ability not only assists the bat in locating a host, it may enable the vampire to locate warm body parts having a rich blood supply close to the surface of the skin. Once a site has been selected, especially sensitive whiskers and sensory organs on the nose pad, upper lip, and elsewhere on the face, allow the vampire to maintain intimate contact with its prey. This highly developed sense of touch anticipates the slightest hint of arousal in the host and allows the bat to alter its behavior accordingly. By way of contrast, the vampire's sense of taste is poorly developed -- hardly a surprise given the bat's singular diet.

Strength and Endurance: Vampires are amazingly strong for their size. Studies have shown that these bats can carry up to a third of their body weight without any apparent difficulty, and that at least some individuals can still fly after having ingested their own weight in purloined blood. Females not only perform these feats, but can do so when burdened with a near-term fetus weighing up to 1/4 of her weight.

Quick in its movements, the vampire bat possesses as much vim as vigor. Those that handle a vampire bat had best be on constant guard. A slight relaxation of one's grip, or a split-second of inattention, can result in the nimble animal wiggling its way into a position from which it can inflict a nasty bite. Bat biologist Ronnie Sidner, who after handling more than 30,000 bats in the field, found her first vampire bat to be so "loose in the skin" that "despite my usually effective grip, the bat managed to move in such a way that there was suddenly a beautiful slice out of the glove I wore -- a cowhide glove of course." In regards to the vampire bat's stamina, Walter Dalquest described the difficulties he experienced while trying to kill these animals for specimens:

> Most mammal collectors kill live bats by placing their index finger against a bat's back, thumb on its chest, and asphyxiating the animal by squeezing. This method is not recommended for vampires. They are so tenacious of life that they can survive several minutes of hard squeezing, time enough to exhaust the muscles of the fingers; and apparently dead animals that had been so treated often recovered. Fruit-eating bats of equal size or larger were quickly killed by pressures that seemed to have little effect on vampires.
>
> Vampires display similar toughness when shot. A charge of shot sufficient to kill large fruit bats almost instantly did not kill vampires unless they were actually struck in the hearts or heads...

My own, more limited, experience supports Dalquest's evaluation of the vampire's tenacity to life.

FEEDING BEHAVIOR

To me it is equally mysterious how the vampires continue to keep alive, if it be really true that they live solely from blood. Special regions of the Amazon forest contain hundreds of thousands of these creatures. The human life in these forests would certainly not suffice to keep a hundredth of this number alive. Contrary to popular supposition the ordinary animal life in the jungle is far from rich, and it would certainly not be sufficient to provide nourishment for the vast numbers of vampires which exist. It seems certain that the vampire bats must be able to go for long periods without food, or else they, like their more uninteresting cousins, the ordinary bats, must also be able to assimilate fruit and insects.

William Montgomery McGovern, *Jungle Paths and Inca Ruins,* 1927

Prey: McGovern's hypothesis notwithstanding, the vampire's diet *is* almost exclusively warm blood. But what animals vampire bats fed upon in pre-Columbian times is a matter for speculation. Early explorers reported vampire bats to be locally abundant in parts of the Amazon Basin and in other equatorial wilderness areas prior to the introduction of livestock. Here, these bats were said to feed on capybaras, deer, peccaries, tapirs, fowls, and humans. Biologists have also observed vampire bats on guano islands immediately off the Peruvian and Chilean coasts feeding on sea birds and nipping on the flippers and ears of sea lions. The distinctive wounds of vampires have even been noticed on fruit-eating bats and reptiles. Without definite knowledge, one can only suspect that guanacos, tapirs, deer, monkeys, large rodents, and people were the vampire's native prey, even though few of these species now ever show signs of having been bitten by these bats.

Whatever its natural hosts, the introduction of domestic animals was a great boon to the common vampire. Many vampire colonies, perhaps most, now feed entirely on the blood of livestock. Although these bats apparently choose to feed on different animals in different areas, analyses of vampire digestive tracts from vampire bat depredation areas in Mexico, Costa Rica, Argentina, and the island of Trinidad show that the selected blood donors in rough order of frequency are cattle (including water buffalo), horses and burros, goats, pigs, poultry, sheep, dogs, and finally, people. The vast majority of the vampire's victims, however, are cattle, horses, and burros. By regularly feeding on prey up to 10,000 times its size, and by not killing their victims, vampire bats are more parasite than predator -- a singular distinction among warm-blooded animals.

Sometimes insects and pieces of meat are found in vampire bat stomachs. These items may be the result of fighting with or grooming fellow vampires, although the finding of an occasional caterpillar could indicate a more varied diet than has heretofore been suspected. Another possibility is that the bats occasionally swallow the piece of flesh removed from a wound prior to partaking of their blood meal. Likewise, the odd record of digested seeds and plant pulp found in vampire bat droppings might indicate that these bats feed on fruit in rare instances. None of these items can be of much importance, however, as the vampire bat's gullet is so narrow, and its stomach so lacking in muscle, as to almost preclude the passage of solid food.

Captive common vampires have fed on the blood of a wide variety of animals offered to them, comprising not only mammals, but birds, reptiles, and amphibians. Some of the more exotic species included porcupines, armadillos, crocodiles, water turtles, lizards, and snakes. However, when small carnivorous mammals such as raccoons, coatis, skunks, and opossums were placed in cages with vampires, the bats themselves were killed and eaten when they attempted to feed on these animals. Cave rats, animals that live in the same caverns as vampires, also fought back vigorously when attacked by the bats. In one case described by Arthur Greenhall, both combatants rose up on their hind legs and engaged in a fist-fight, the rat using its forepaws, the bat its folded wings and thumbs. When the rat was put in with two bats, the rodent was subdued and killed. Captive vampire bats only showed scars and other evidence of being fed upon by other vampires when the bats were deprived of food and unable to escape. Although these experiments were conducted in the laboratory and have no application to natural conditions, they show that vampires are unlikely to successfully feed on alert, aggressive animals. The risk involved, and the decreased chance for a meal, probably explain why dogs are not attacked more often.

Common vampire bats can and do prey on birds, but further investigations into depredations on poultry often show the culprit to be either a hairy-legged or a white-winged vampire. Both of these species are more adept at climbing trees than the common vampire bat and more prone to feed on bird blood. In one experiment, captive hairy-legged vampires refused to take mammal blood and would only feed on chickens. These bats landed on the chicken's back and proceeded to crawl head-first down to the vent where they sometimes drew enough blood to kill the bird. The white-winged vampire feeds on perching birds by climbing up to them head first and carefully biting them on the toes, legs, vent, or lower breast. Captives of this species nonetheless

44

have taken the blood of donkeys, goats, and guinea-pigs, and wild white-winged vampires are known to feed on cattle and goats. This ability to feed on mammals as well as birds has caused some biologists to speculate that this vampire may be in the midst of changing its diet from bird blood to the more reliable supply found in large domestic mammals.

Hunting Methods: It has long been recognized that vampire bats tend to repeatedly attack the same victim night after night while ignoring other animals in the same pasture or corral. The animal's location as well as its color also is thought to be a factor. A study by Dennis Turner in Costa Rica showed that cattle at the edge of a herd were selected more often than those in the middle, and that livestock pastured in wooded areas seemed to be more vulnerable than those in open fields. Turner also found that grazing animals were less likely to be victimized than those which were bedded down. Once a prey animal has been selected, even the use of electric lights, which normally discourage vampires, often fails to keep a determined bat from obtaining a meal. Nor is the selection of a particular host an individual preference. Arthur Greenhall observed as many as twelve bats on one cow during a single night, and reported a steer that was attacked no less than 30 times between nightfall and dawn!

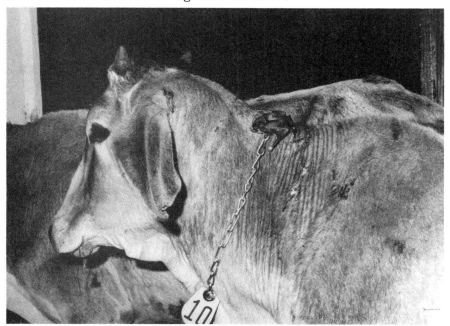

Figure 24. Vampire bat preparing to bite a Zebu calf. The scars on the calf are the result of previous bites. U.S. Fish and Wildlife Service photo by Richard J. Burns courtesy of Clay Mitchell.

On finding a potential host, the vampire bat hovers overhead, flying back and forth, until it chooses a method of attack. The bat's normal *modus operandi* is to gently and silently land either on the targeted animal's back, mane, or tail, or on the ground nearby -- a feat these bats perform well. Once on a cow or other animal, the vampire crawls head downward in search of a vulnerable location to make its bite. Should the bat have landed on the ground, it will tippy-toe up to its intended victim with the utmost stealth. After much exploratory sniffing, an assailable location is found, and the vampire begins licking the hair on the intended feeding site. Regardless of how much care is employed, such attention does not always go unnoticed. Cows may flick their tails or ears in an attempt to dislodge a bat, and mules have been known to throw themselves on their backs in their efforts to dislodge these winged tormentors. Should the tail switch too close, or a hoof be raised preparatory to a kick, the vampire deftly avoids the blow or jumps off the animal. Usually though, the host appears unaware of, or indifferent to, the bat's activities. And, the vampire is nothing if not persistent. If forced to retreat, it hovers about, waiting to return at the first opportunity. Only after its appetite is sated does the vampire slide off the animal and fly away. Should the bat have consumed so much blood that it is unable to take-off, it may back its way up a tree or other structure until it either reaches sufficient height to launch itself into flight or assimilates enough of its meal to again become air-borne.

The Vampire's Bite

It is a disputed point as to the manner in which the bat makes the incision; whether with its tongue, with the sharp nail of its thumb, or by boring with one of its long canine teeth by flying around in a circle.

Charles Waterton, *Wanderings in South America*, 1885

When making a bite, the vampire bat invariably selects a site where blood is close to the surface of the skin. Large animals approached from the ground are commonly bitten in the cleft at the back of the hoof or foot. Should the bat have landed on the back of a cow, horse, or burro, it will usually work its way forward to attack the animal on the shoulder or the back of the neck. Bites are also common on the nose and ears, and on water buffaloes, inside the nostrils. Several observers, beginning with Cabeza de Vaca in the 16th Century, have remarked that the teats on pigs may sometimes be so scarified from past bites that their piglets are unable to suckle. Poultry are most often bitten between the toes, on the comb, neck, leg, or vent. Toes are the site of most bites on humans, although the tip of the nose and ears are also common targets. Should a previous wound be present, the vampire will seek it out. Once a wound is present, it may be used by several bats, as an earlier bite can be reopened in a few minutes instead of the half-hour or more needed to locate a new site and open a fresh wound.

The vampire may employ one of three types of bites to open the skin and obtain its blood meal. The most common method is to lick the fur and turn it aside, and then use its razor sharp upper incisors and canines to slice downward into the flesh. At the same time the lobed lower incisors gently grasp the surface of the skin. A divot of skin and flesh about 1/8 of an inch in diameter is then surgically excised. Such crater-like wounds are distinctive and readily recognized by an experienced person.

Figure 25. Vampire bat attacking the hock area of a cow. Note the bat's upright posture. U.S. Fish and Wildlife Service photo courtesy of Clay Mitchell.

Should the blood be especially close to the surface, or a previous wound be present, the vampire may merely inflict a quick scratch on the skin with the upper incisors, or rasp the area open with the rough tip and sides of its tongue. The time required to select a site, open a wound, and draw blood may vary from under ten minutes to 40 minutes or more, but is usually about 20 minutes. If the vampire is experienced at his work, none of these procedures will cause pain sufficient to alert the host.

After a wound is opened, the vampire inserts its tongue through the space between the two lower incisors and along the groove in the lower lip. Two channels on the underside of the tongue draw blood from the wound in the same manner as a drinking straw. As a ribbon of blood begins to flow, the bat draws the fluid up with its long pink tongue. The action of flicking the tongue in and out at a rate of four darts a second results in the animal's head taking on a peculiar nodding motion. The common vampire bat does not suck blood in the ordinary sense, nor does it lap it up like a cat feeding from a saucer of milk; it sips *and* licks blood. And lick it up it does. A normal meal will exceed 2/3 of an ounce of the fluid, the equivalent of from 40 to 60 percent of the vampire's weight. Nor is it unusual for a hungry vampire bat to drink its own weight or more, and starving individuals have been known to draw up to two ounces of blood from a victim.

While the blood is being drawn up the bottom of the tongue, saliva is flowing down a grove on the tongue's upper surface. The tongue is periodically swirled into the wound, further mixing the saliva with the blood. Although it was long thought that the vampire's saliva must contain an anesthetic to deaden the pain and prevent the donor from being aroused, no study has shown this to be so. The vampire's saliva may, however, contain an ingredient that inhibits blood vessels from contracting, and it is definitely known to contain a powerful anti-coagulant that prevents the host's blood from clotting. So potent is this anticoagulant that it is not uncommon for a wound to bleed freely for up to a half hour, plenty of time for the vampire to partake its fill.

Desmokinase: Scientists have long wondered how the vampire can obtain its liquid meal without the blood clotting. For an animal to survive even a mild wound, any blood leaving the circulatory system must coalesce or clot to prevent hemorrhaging to death. This essential process is not only chemically complex, it is highly efficient. A normal wound of the same size as the vampire bat inflicts would cease bleeding in one or two minutes. Yet, the vampire requires prolonged and copious bleeding to finish its meal. It wasn't until a series of experiments were conducted on captive vampires in London in the 1960s that scientists learned how the vampire overcomes this formidable obstacle.

Clotting depends upon the blood plasma producing an insoluble substance called fibrin. As a defense against the unwanted build-up of fibrin in the bloodstream, the plasma also contains a protein known as plasminogen. Normally inactive, plasminogen produces enzymes which dissolve blood clots and prevent thrombosis. To combat fibrin and the blood-clotting mechanism, the vampire bat's saliva contains two plasminogen activators, the most important of which is an enzyme termed *Desmokinase*. Saliva containing *Desmokinase* is mixed into the wound by the bat licking the skin prior to biting, when it flows down the top of the tongue, and by swirling the tongue in the open wound. Interestingly, studies have shown that *Desmokinase* is a a specific activator only for the plasminogens found in the blood of certain mammals including cattle, members of the horse family, and people. Sheep and dog blood are relatively unaffected. Because *Desmokinase* breaks down the clotting action of human blood, some scientists believe it may have some promise as a means of preventing strokes.

Much less is known about the bite of the hairy-legged and white-winged vampires. The former appears to feed primarily on large birds and the latter seems to prefer smaller perching birds. Like the common vampire on a cow, the hairy-legged commonly lands quietly on a bird's back and then creeps downward headfirst to make its incision. No one has actually witnessed the biting action of a hairy-leg, but it appears that this bat's unusually lobed lower front teeth are used to grip the bird's skin in much the same manner employed by the common vampire. Unlike the common vampire, however, this species is said to be a true blood-sucker, the bat using its lips to form a seal over the wound.

Other Adaptations For Feeding On Blood: Vampires are the only mammals that *can* subsist entirely on blood. There are good reasons for this. Such a diet poses several problems, not the least of which is that blood is difficult to digest -- even carnivores such as dogs quickly become sick if fed only blood. Fresh blood is also 90% water and heavy in weight. What isn't water is almost pure protein -- blood contains no fat and virtually no carbohydrates. With only a protein diet, an animal has a difficult time storing energy. To accommodate the demands imposed by its blood fare, the vampire must not only have a specialized mouth, lips, and tongue, it must possess a digestive system and intestinal bacteria that can process this unusual food, and be able to assimilate and dispose of huge quantities of liquid within a relatively short period of time.

The vampire's digestive and excretory systems are wonderfully adapted to meet these exigencies. Ingested blood quickly fills both the tubular stomach and large intestine. Besides having thin, elastic walls, the highly expandable "T"-shaped stomach contains a large secondary pouch for even greater storage and absorption of fluid. This ability to ingest large amounts of blood gives the vampire a spherical, bloated appearance after feeding. Indeed, some of the bats become so engorged that they have difficulty taking off, and are forced to spend several hours in some secondary retreat digesting their purloined meals before returning home.

Because blood meals contain large amounts of nitrogen as well as water, the bat must pass a large volume of urine over a short period of time. This function is admirably served, not only by the animal's oddly shaped stomach which possesses a special network of small blood vessels, but by its large liver, pancreas and oversize kidneys which rapidly assimilate fluids and concentrate nutrients. The resulting large amount of urine necessitates an almost immediate need to pass water after feeding, and the vampire responds by releasing a copious flow of urine equivalent to about 1/4 of the meal's volume. This urination occurs within an hour of commencing its meal -- sometimes while the bat is still feeding. From four to six hours later the bat passes another 1/4 of the meal's volume as highly concentrated urine.

At least partially because of their sole diet of blood, vampire bats are also presented with some unique temperature and water balance problems. Without fat reserves, these bats have difficulty maintaining their normal body temperature of around 98.6 degrees F. when the outside thermometer falls below 50 degrees F. Cold, rainy nights and low temperatures are therefore avoided as the vampire cannot afford to get wet and chilled. Should its body temperature drop to 72 degrees F., the bat cannot rewarm itself, and vampires will die if subjected to air temperatures below 35 or 40 degrees for only a few days. At the other end of the spectrum, vampires must avoid ambient temperatures above 86 degrees F. due to their high rate of metabolism and poor ability to cool themselves. The bats cannot tolerate 90 degree temperatures for any length of time, and even a few minutes of exposure to a temperature of 100 degrees is lethal.

The vampire bat's high metabolic rate exacerbates an already high water and weight loss. Indeed, the vampire's water evaporation rate is among the highest recorded for any mammal, and partially explains why the animal seeks out daytime roosts having high humidities. So great is the average rate of weight loss, that without eating, a vampire will lose 20% of its weight during a normal day. Just two hours of active foraging without locating a meal causes an 11% drop in weight -- a potentially devastating reduction as the bat cannot recover should its weight drop by 25%. On cold days, and during the dry season, the vampire's metabolic rate and food requirements are even greater. Without a fresh supply of blood, this critical level is reached in only 60 to 70 hours. Vampires therefore cannot go two consecutive nights without feeding. If a vampire bat does not obtain a blood meal within that time, it starves to death.

THE VAMPIRE BAT AT HOME

Flying fish skimmed in all directions and vampires (*Desmodus rufus*) in scores flew from the dead branches projecting from the water. They choose a small-sized one, say two inches in diameter, and alight, one below the other, with heads raised, watching us. Like little animated sun-dials, they revolve on their perches as the sun passes over, keeping the wood between them and the bright light. Many of the snags had bits of dead leaves and other debris clinging to them, brought down and lodged by the last freshet, and it was not until we almost put our hand on them and the bats flew, that we could tell whether we were looking at a cluster of vampires or dead leaves. There were hundreds throughout the course of the river [in Venezuela], so it is a widespread diurnal roosting habit of these fierce little creatures.

Mary and William Beebe, *Our Search For A Wilderness*, 1910

The Vampire Bat at Rest: More than 80 percent of the vampire bat's time is spent sleeping or resting in a cave, mine or hollow tree. A preferred roost is one that provides semi to total darkness, has a relatively constant temperature between 78 and 82 degrees F., and comes with a high humidity (100% is not too much). If such a recess is available, the bats prefer to roost on a rough surface within 100 yards of the cavity's mouth or entrance. Although vampires are able to hang from their hind feet like other bats, they prefer a surface that they can also grip with their thumbnails. Thus, the bat's body is held close to the chamber's walls, allowing the animal to scuttle off on foot in any direction it desires. When moving about, the common vampire climbs and descends vertical walls while in a head-down position. Should the vampire bats be disturbed, the animals will either secret themselves inside fissures, or fly to more distant recesses, crying and squeaking as they flee. Rarely can one be driven outside of its chosen daytime haven.

Nighttime Activity: Vampire bats leave their roosts as soon as it is completely dark, flying close (sometimes as close as a few inches) to the ground. The bats postpone their foraging, however, if the moon is up. This desire for complete darkness is thought to be due to the need to avoid bat falcons and other predators rather than to any possibility that the vampire bat's hosts are more vulnerable on dark nights. Researchers have found no correlation between the vampire's ability to obtain a blood meal and the phase of the moon. Once on the wing, the actual foraging time for a female vampire bat averages only about two hours; males are gone from their roost even less -- only about 90 minutes. An analysis of stomachs from nearly 600 vampire bats caught just before dawn in Mexico showed that older bats were more successful in obtaining blood than young ones. Only ten percent of vampire bats more than two-years-old failed to find a meal, while a third of the bats under two-years-old went home with empty stomachs.

Figure 26. Vampire bat pathway near Minas Nuevas, Sonora, Mexico. Mist nets located close to the ground resulted in capturing several vampire bats as they passed *below* and between the foliage of the trees. Photo by author.

Movements and Home Ranges: Lengthy travels are avoided, and information from radio-equipped vampires in Mexico has shown the average distance that a bat flies during the night is less than three miles. The chosen pasture is often within a mile of the roost, and rarely do the bats travel more than five miles to feed. In a few cases their hosts were as far as 12 miles away, requiring the bats to make a 24-mile round trip. Hence, most vampire bats hunt in the area of their home roost and rarely trespass on another colony's feeding grounds.

Vampire bats apparently have either a relatively well developed homing instinct or good memories. In one study, William Wimsatt transported and released a number of vampire bats at various distances from their roost site. All of the bats released within 10 miles of their roost found their way home within two nights. Two vampire bats released 18 miles away were never seen again.

More impressive movements have been reported over longer periods of time, and one vampire bat in Argentina is known to have moved 60 miles from its banding site. Seasonal movements of this essentially non-migratory animal have also been documented, and at least some populations are believed to use different roost sites in winter than in summer. Northern populations do not appear to go south for the winter, however. Vampire bats were captured in late November in the same mine shafts near Alamos, Sonora, at the northern limits of their distribution, that they occupied in July and August.

SOCIAL BEHAVIOR

> South America makes up for its lack, relatively to Africa and India, of large man-eating carnivores by the extraordinary ferocity or bloodthirstiness of certain small creatures of which the kinsfold elsewhere are harmless. It is only here that fish no bigger than trout kill swimmers, and bats the size of the ordinary "flittermice" of the northern hemisphere drain the life-blood of big beasts and of man himself.

> President Theodore Roosevelt, *Through the Brazilian Wilderness*, 1914

Vampire bats are social animals. Roosting groups vary from a few individuals inhabiting trees and crevices to colonies of up to 5000 clustered together in a cave or abandoned mine. The typical vampire bat colony, however, contains somewhere between a dozen and 50 bats, composed of an adult male and eight to twenty adult females and their young. Although as many as 45 different kinds of bats, including the other two species of vampires, have been reported to be present in the same cave or mine, these species invariably roost in a different chamber than the common vampire bat. The members of the vampire bat colony, however, know their roostmates well.

Even though vampire bat populations appear to be about equally divided between the sexes, the numbers of males and females in any given roost may be highly skewed. Each colony commonly contains an adult male who takes up a position between several females and the entrance to the hollow tree or cavern. Bachelor males commonly roost together, either in another part of the tree or tunnel, or in a separate roost site. Nonetheless, each male aggressively protects his own small area of turf from other males whether females are present or not. This pugnacious behavior often results in young males from twelve to 18 months of age having to take up quarters a mile or more away from their parent roost. Sometimes these expulsions are only accomplished by force on the part of the dominant male or "roostmaster" who may maintain his preferential location and status for several years.

The usual scenario is for the roostmaster to fly to the nearest pasture to feed, and then immediately return home. Bachelor males, on the other hand, frequently spend much of the night searching out new roosts, presumably in the hope of finding a colony of females whose roostmaster is out feeding. Females have their own feeding pattern. Often foraging in pairs or with their flying young, it is not unusual for these *vampiras* to use two or more secondary roost sites after they have finished feeding. Female vampire bats may also use more than one daytime or "homeroost," even though they have a strong attachment to the colony to which they belong. Female members of a colony may roost together for 10 years or more, despite the fact that most *vampiras* change roost locations every couple of years or so. For some reason, perhaps because of a need for a more favorable humidity or temperature, too many parasites, or a lack of prey, the entire colony will change location. Prime sites are rarely vacant, however, and a favorite roost site will often be reoccupied within days, even if all of the vampire bats in it are removed.

Figure 27. Roosting vampire bat colony. U.S. Fish and Wildlife Service photo courtesy of Clay Mitchell.

Vampire bats are unique in the animal world in that certain individuals donate food by regurgitating blood to colony members. In an amazing study of both captive and wild animals, Gerald Wilkinson discovered that the bats who share food are not always related to each other. Although most food sharing is between mothers and their pups, some females will feed another bat's youngster and even another adult. Such communal feeding is important to the vampire bat's survival as these bats will die if deprived of food for 60 to 70 hours. A social kinship therefore develops between those bats that share food. Wilkinson found that a vampire bat which was fed when it failed to find a meal remembered which bat gave it blood, and reciprocated the favor at a later date. The amount of blood given depended more on the recipient's needs than on any filial relationship. Adult males were never fed by other bats, although males sometimes fed females and young within the colony, prompting Wilkinson to conclude that these males were bartering blood for later sexual favors!

Approximately two hours of the vampire bat's day is spent grooming itself or its roostmates. Much of this licking and biting is an attempt to diminish the numerous parasites that infest these animals, but a good amount of socializing also seems to be involved. A typical grooming session involves more than 250 body contacts and appears to be a form of kinship bonding between females. A *vampira* buddy-system is thus formed in which two or more females regularly share blood. These sessions involve not only much licking and fondling, but are accompanied by faint squeaks and begging cries. Grooming continues until the blood is exchanged, the donor periodically feeling the recipient's stomach during regurgitation to determine its fullness. Wilkinson thought that these activities allowed the donor bat to detect "cheaters" -- bats who had failed to share a meal when they were approached. Cheaters, when it came their turn to solicit blood, were repulsed and fought-off by their "sisters."

After dark, adult female vampire bats frequently depart their day roost in pairs or in small groups of up to a half dozen. Similar small contingents have also been observed to arrive simultaneously at a feeding site and circle the intended prey *en masse*. And, while the usual sequence is for a vampire bat to hunt once a night, a female will sometimes lead other of her roost-mates to a cow pasture where she had fed earlier in the evening. After the other bats have fed, all of the *vampiras* will then return to the roost together. It thus appears that one or more females in a colony take on the role of being a "big sister," leading unsuccessful roostmates to a proven feeding pasture or victim.

Social interactions have also been observed among vampire bats in the act of feeding. Females and their yearling young may drink together from the same wound, and as many as seven bats have been seen to sequentially take blood from a single wound as if some sort of pecking order were involved. Antagonistic behavior usually only occurs when two adults try to drink from the same wound at the same time. Such encounters involve a great deal of hair-bristling, wing-beating, and lunging accompanied by audible shrieks. If the altercation involves a male and a female, victory most often goes to the larger female.

Adult females may not only also successfully defend an entire prey animal, some of the *vampiras* in a colony may act in a group to defend an especially lucrative pasture or feeding area from another colony's vampire bats.

When the roost-master is not out foraging, he remains at his post close to the roost entrance. Any male that tries to enter when the master is at home is likely to be attacked, the two bats screaming at each other and displaying the same aggressive responses used to defend a wound on which one of the bats is feeding. If neither of the combatants gives way, a vicious fight ensues with much parrying and biting. These battles may last for several minutes to throughout the night, and must be fairly common as most adult males display scars and wounds. Arthur Greenhall once observed a vanquished male fleeing a roost in broad daylight after a particularly brutal confrontation.

Hairy-legged vampires, while sometimes occupying the same caves as common vampire bats, are more likely to be found as solitary individuals or in pairs. When a colony of hairy-legged vampires is found, the comparatively few bats present tend to be more scattered and less cohesive than colonies of common vampire bats. Quiet and gentle, this species is also less likely to flee than its more numerous cousin and is less disturbed by light.

White-winged vampires have been found in colonies of up to 30 or so bats, and appear to be, if anything, even more aggressive than common vampires. These bats vigorously defend poultry and other prey against others of their kind, and individual whitewings have been reported to defend larger territories than common vampire bats. This species is also reported to be less skittish about flashlights than its more common cousin.

SEX LIFE AND REPRODUCTION

While the sun had been setting, a baby was born. Blind and hairless, it fell into a cradle formed by membrane between its mother's legs. Instinctively, it chirped through milk teeth while its mother spread her baby's wings and sniffed scent glands that would distinguish it from all other infants in the dark. Only then did she allow it to climb to a waiting nipple. As it fed, she watched with bright eyes and oversize ears as the rest of the colony stirred from their torpor. Life was spreading. In the next niche, a male wrapped his wings around a female, his stomach to her back and his teeth dug into the nape of her neck, copulating...

Martin Cruz Smith, *Nightwing*, 1977

Both male and female vampire bats become sexually mature when they are about a year old. But unlike African wild dogs and other communal mammals that participate in food-sharing, all of the mature females in a colony come into heat and breed. Sexual activity, however, may not always be confined to the day roost where any subordinate males present are separated from the roost-master and his females by a distance of at least three yards. Although the roost-master engages in most of the breeding activity, his access to the harem is by no means exclusive. Should the roost-master be out foraging, other males will take advantage of his absence, and females in a colony occasionally visit other roost sites during the night. There are therefore plenty of opportunities to be "unfaithful," and subordinate males do almost half of the breeding.

Because adult females are larger than males, the female is able to repulse any unwanted attention by either scrambling away from his advances, or, if necessary, attacking an undesired suitor with bared fangs and claws. Should she be receptive, the male grasps the female from behind and clasps her flanks tightly with his folded wings. To secure her further, he then grasps the fur on her neck with his teeth. The actual act of copulation only lasts from one to three minutes after which the female's vagina is sealed with a plug of semen. Upon fertilization, a single embryo (rarely two) begins developing as soon as the egg is implanted in the uterus.

Mating may take place at any time throughout the year, even though there is some evidence that breeding activity is seasonally synchronized. A study at La Selva, Costa Rica, showed that young bats were only born during the spring dry season, and collections of vampire bats in Jalisco, Mexico, indicated most pregnancies occurred from January through May. Most of the young bats on Trinidad are born in the spring and fall, during the spring in Argentina, and at other times elsewhere.

Gestation is long -- from 205 to 220 days, or about seven months. By way of contrast, the duration of labor is short, only about three minutes of pulsing and thrusting. The baby is born while its mother hangs head down, clutching the ceiling or wall of the roost with her feet and thumbs. Arriving with functional eyes, pinkish wings, and nearly hairless, the pup, as baby vampire bats are called, is remarkably active. Almost immediately, the pup climbs up on its mother and begins to suckle while its umbilical cord is still attached. Both the pup and its mother are now thoroughly licked by other female members of the colony. These attentions to mother and pup continue for several weeks, the mother also being fed regurgitated blood which she soon shares with her pup. By passing this regurgitated blood on to her offspring, the mother assures that the colony's newest member will have the microbes necessary to digest what will one day be its only fare. These meals supplement the pup's diet of mother's milk for several months. Orphaned pups may also be adopted if a nursing female is available -- a behavior limited to very few mammals.

The growth of the infant is comparatively slow and the dependency period is long. Weighing from five to seven grams at birth, the pup's weight doubles in about 20 to 25 days, during which time it clings to the mother's nipple. If the mother's forays afield are close to home, she may even carry her offspring with her, the pup clinging to her body. After about two months of age, the increasingly heavy pup is stashed with the colony's other youngsters, leaving the mother to go forth on her nightly rounds unencumbered. Should the colony be disturbed in its roost, those pups too big to carry, and too young to fly, are abandoned by their flighty parents.

At three months of age, the pup has attained the dimensions but not the weight of an adult. The pup begins to fly at around four months of age and soon begins to accompany its mother on her nightly forays. Milk and regurgitated blood are still an important part of the youngster's diet, however, and weaning is not complete until the young bat is about ten months old.

Mothers may mate again as soon as 45 days after giving birth, and the average interval between births is just under a year. The bond between the mother and her young is nonetheless surprisingly long-lasting, and it is not unusual for a mother to be suckling two young of different age-classes at the same time.

Little is known about the breeding habits of the hairy-legged vampire bat other than that nursery colonies of this species tend to contain few animals. The breeding season in this species may also be better defined than in the common vampire bat. At least most young hairy-legged vampires in Mexico are born in early summer. Even less is known about the breeding habits of the white-winged vampire bat. About the only information available on this species is that captive pairs display a strong devotion to each other. This would suggest that white-winged vampires have strong pair bonds and do not engage in polygamous or promiscuous mating behavior.

ENEMIES, LONGEVITY, AND MORTALITY

> Before falling asleep on my camp-bed on the veranda, I noticed a number of vampires circling round me, and, pondering in the safe shelter of my mosquito net the difficulty the creatures must have in obtaining their daily ration of blood, slid gently down the steps of oblivion to a gradual diminuendo of Lewis Carroll's classical speculation, 'Do cats

eat bats?' or, pregnant with meaning at Uchiza, 'Do bats eat cats?'

Christopher Sandeman, *A Forgotten River,*
1939

Because vampire bats only go forth in total darkness, their natural enemies are few. Owls probably take an occasional vampire bat as do predatory bats. Should a vampire venture forth too early in the evening, or return too late in the morning, it risks being bagged by a bat falcon or a hawk. Vampire bats are easy meat in daylight; biologists have observed such inefficient predators as great-tailed grackles and brown jays overtaking and killing vampire bats released from nets after sunrise. When in their roosts, however, the bats are relatively secure. Carnivorous bats, owls, and snakes have even been observed in the same caverns without the vampire bats being molested. More dangerous to vampire bats are several blood-borne diseases and man's efforts to control them, both of which have decimated local vampire bat populations. Starvation is also a constant threat and probably represents the most common cause of death in vampire bats. Cattle and other livestock are periodically rounded up and removed from the vampire's feeding areas, forcing the bats to find a new food source *pronto.*

Vampire bats must also contend with their own blood-sucking pests. These include bat flies, mites, fleas, chigger larvae, and ticks but not lice or blood-sucking bugs. So unusual is it for a vampire bat *not* to have insects clinging to its skin or fur, that one of the reasons postulated for a colony changing its roost location is to reduce the parasite load. Parasites may also influence a colony's size as individuals in large colonies tend to have more parasites than members of smaller groups.

Vampire bats are potentially long-lived animals. Individuals have lived 19 years in captivity, and growth rings on the teeth indicate that some wild vampires live nearly as long. With such a potentially long life, and assuming a pup every ten to twelve months, it is possible for a female to produce up to 20 youngsters during her lifetime.

Banding studies by Gerald Wilkinson in an area with abundant prey in Costa Rica showed that about three-fourths of the adult vampire bats survived from one year to the next -- an annual loss of 25%. More than half of the young vampires under a year old did not survive their first year of life. Other studies have shown similar mortality rates and a high loss of juveniles. The greater mortality of juveniles is believed to be due to their inexperience at inflicting painless, undetectable bites. When a vampire bat is detected in the act of opening a wound the prey is alerted and the bat's chances for a blood meal are much reduced. If it were not for the sharing of regurgitated blood by older comrades, the mortality of young vampires would be even higher. Wilkinson estimated that without food-sharing more than 80 percent of a colony's vampire bats would fail to make it through the year. Because of food-sharing, more than half of the bats survive, and the size of an undisturbed colony remains relatively stable.

PART II VAMPIRES AND PEOPLE

VAMPIRE BAT ATTACKS ON HUMANS

> The governor was bitten by one of those animals while he was asleep in a brigantine, one of his feet being uncovered. All night the blood kept on flowing, till he woke from feeling his leg cold, and finding the bed soaked with blood, thought somebody had wounded him; but those on board searched for the place where he was wounded, and when they found what they knew, by experience, to be the bite of a bat, they laughed. The governor found that a slice of his toe had been bitten off. These bats always bite where there is a vein...
>
> Alvar Nuñez Cabeza de Vaca, 1555

Even in localities where vampire bats are abundant, attacks on humans are relatively infrequent. People who camp out overnight in undisturbed forests are sometimes bitten, as are persons living in small villages along rivers where livestock and vampire bats tend to concentrate. Even where these bats are abundant, it is unusual for more than one or two villagers to claim that they have been bitten by a vampire bat, some of them bearing disfiguring scars as proof.

A sudden removal of the vampire bat's regular hosts might cause vampire bats to attack people. In 1975, Tim McCarthy observed an increase in the number of Indians bitten in two Maya villages in Belize after all of the local pigs had been slaughtered in an anti-hog cholera campaign. In a similar case in the early 1980s, Indians in two villages in Peru were subjected to an unprecedented number of vampire bat attacks after all of the local pigs had been killed for destroying planted crops. There are other examples, involving other kinds of livestock.

Some people, including vampire bat biologist Clay Mitchell, have observed that vampire bat attacks on humans seem to increase with the advent of the rainy season, or during periods of unusually wet or dry weather. The implication of these observations is that weather changes can either trigger an influx of new vampire bats into an area, or that the bats' usual hosts become unavailable as cattle are rounded up and moved to other pastures. Either way, the vampires' normal feeding patterns are disturbed, and the bats are forced to find an alternate food source.

The often reported observation that native peoples are more prone to be bitten by vampire bats than visiting Americans and

61

Europeans also has an explanation. This apparent preference for dark skinned flesh is not due to any prejudice on the part of the bats, but to the greater vulnerability of the natives' dwellings and to their greater likelihood of exposure. Many Indians live in palm-thatched and stick-walled houses that allow bats easy access to the occupants, and rural laborers are more likely to sleep in the jungle without the protection of tents or netting.

For some of these same reasons, and probably because of their deeper slumber, children are also bitten more often than adults -- a phenomenon noted by several people who have studied vampire bats, including Arthur Greenhall in Trinidad, Clay Mitchell in Nicaragua, B.B. Nehaul in Guyana, and Tim McCarthy in Belize. Several of these investigators have also reported instances of a particular child being repeatedly bitten over several days while other people (and animals) in the same house went unmolested. Arthur Greenhall tells of one small girl being bitten numerous times in one night while her brother slept undisturbed, and Merlin Tuttle observed a four-year-old Indian boy in Peru who had been bitten 14 times on the crown of his shaved head.

Figure 28. Maya dwelling within tropical deciduous forest in Yucatán, Mexico. The cactus-rib walls and thatched roof allow the entry of vampire bats. Photo by author.

Why the bats showed a decided preference for these individuals is somewhat of an enigma. Perhaps these children were more prone to attack than their siblings because of where they slept. A more likely

62

explanation, however, is that once a vampire bat has opened a wound, the animal finds a repeat performance more promising of success than beginning anew. A second helping also takes less time to prepare as attested to by observations of vampire bats feeding on livestock.

The tendency for vampire bats to attack native children is by no means exclusive, however. Numerous American and European travelers have been bitten by these bats, some of them repeatedly. Archaeologist Thomas Gann received numerous bites on the foot, neck, and nose while camped out one night near Copán, Honduras.

Figure 29. Typical vampire bat wound on a man's toe. U.S. Fish and Wildlife Service photo courtesy of Clay Mitchell.

Toes, noses, the tips of ears, and other extremities are the usual targets, although people are frequently also bitten on the face and other exposed parts of the body. Hairy areas are generally avoided. The great explorer-biologist Alfred Russel Wallace was bitten on the heel, and concluded that other than "the curiosity of the thing, to be bitten by a bat is very disagreeable." He also reported another less than agreeable incident regarding a Negro colleague of his, who after having been repeatedly bitten by vampire bats, "came to us with a doleful countenance, telling us he thought the bats meant to eat him up quite [literally], for having covered up his hands and feet in a blanket, they had descended beneath his hammock of open network, and attacking the most prominent part of his person, had bitten him through a hole in his trousers."

Appearances vary, but the typical bite is a small oval gouge about 1/4 inch long, 1/5 of an inch wide, and 1/10 of an inch deep. When the skin is stretched tight, the wound resembles an oblong shallow trough. Bleeding is usually profuse and prolonged, and, if it were not for the blood, few victims would even realize they had been bitten. A 19th Century explorer, Alfred Simson, tells of conversing with a man in Ecuador "who was remarking that he could not understand how some people always got so unaccountably bitten, though whilst he was actually making this remark, in the dusk, a bat was sucking one of his toes, as was evidenced by the bat being seen by me and himself to flutter away whilst the man's toe, to his great surprise, was found to be bleeding severely."

Needless to say, most, but not all, donors never awake during the bat's operation. This phenomenon, which cannot be duplicated with the sharpest scalpel or needle, has long intrigued scientists and laymen alike. Indeed, the quandary of how the vampire bat can administer such a delicate operation has, and continues to be, the subject of much speculation. Early theories as to the bat's methodology included the belief that the initial opening was made by the bat gently rasping the skin with its pointed tongue or its teeth. Others were of the decided opinion that the bat used its sharp canine tooth to gradually drill a hole in the skin as the bat flew around and around the site of the intended excavation, the fanning motion of the bat's wings inducing an ever deeper slumber in the victim. Still others reasoned that the wound was made by the bat's oddly protruding thumbnail. An even more bizarre hypothesis was that the nose-leaf of another species of bat was somehow used to open the wound, and that once the blood began to flow, the vampire bat partook of the streaming blood!

To solve the riddle of the bat's remarkable stealth, numerous scientists offered themselves up as bait, hoping to record the experience of being bitten while in a conscious state. Alas, the bats invariably refused to cooperate, either failing to appear or preferring instead to attack others of the party who were not "playing possum." Undoubtedly the most publicized attempt to elicit a bite was an effort by the flamboyant tropical biologist and author William Beebe. Beebe, who had his own views as to the nature of the vampire bat's bite, described his experience in his 1925 book, *Edge of the Jungle*. After offering himself up to the bats in total darkness, and feeling what he took to be the stealthy, nearly imperceptible movement of one of these "winged weasels" on his elbow, he decided that:

> ... now was the moment to seize him, call for a lantern, and solve his supersurgical skill, the exact method of this vespertilial anaesthetist. Slowly, very slowly, I lifted the other hand, always thinking of my elbow, so that I might keep

all the muscles relaxed. Very slowly it approached, and with as swift a motion as I could achieve, I grasped at the vampire. I felt a touch of fur and gripped a struggling skinny wing. There came a single nip of teeth, and the wing tip slipped through my fingers. I could detect no trace of blood by feeling, so turned over and went to sleep. In the morning I found a tiny scratch, with the skin barely broken; and heartily disappointed, I realized that my tickling and tingling had been the preliminary symptoms of the operation.

In 1950 animal collector Roderick Campbell claimed to be the first person to successfully induce a vampire bat to bite him while feigning sleep. After the bat landed nearby, it crept up to Campbell's elbow which it bit. Campbell described the bat's administration of the bite as a "slight tingling sensation, as if it [the elbow] were going to sleep." By then, however, thanks to the work of Raymond Ditmars and other scientists, the stalking techniques of the common vampire bat had been well documented. Nonetheless, no matter how sharp its teeth, the ability of the bat to open a wound and extract a blood meal without arousing its human host is simply amazing.

Depredations on Livestock and Pets

The dogs kept by the Indians [in Guiana] lose nearly all their pups, owing to the attacks of vampires. The mothers know how to roll over and to brush off the horrid creature: but they are helpless to save their pups. Our pet would run backwards and forwards, from her yelling pups to our bedroom door, whining for us to come and remove the attacking horror. Fowls must be carefully protected at night in wire-net houses. Calves suffered severely. They became emaciated, and some of them succumbed, ere they could grow to be large enough to withstand the continual lancing.

Reverend Walter G. White, in "The
Vampire's Bite" by William Beebe, 1927

Of more concern to many Latin Americans than the occasional human bite, are vampire bat attacks on their domestic animals. The intensity of these depredations vary considerably by location, but can, and often do, represent a considerable hardship or economic loss. Although cattle are the animals most often attacked, horses, mules, burros, pigs, goats, and poultry are also regularly victimized. Even the more agile dogs and the higher elevation llamas are not immune to attack.

Figure 30. Horse in Nicaragua suffering from repeated attacks by vampire bats. Note the animal's overall poor condition. U.S. Fish and Wildlife Service photo courtesy of Clay Mitchell.

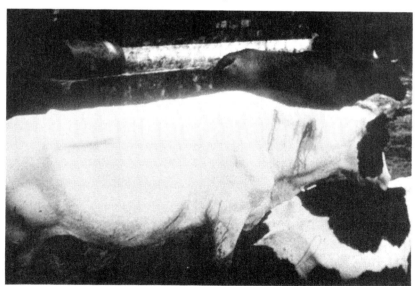

Figure 31. Dairy cow bleeding from several vampire bat bites. U.S. Fish and Wildlife Service photo courtesy of Clay Mitchell.

Nearly all of the conquistadors and early explorers of South and Central America's *tierra caliente* complained of their mounts and transport animals being bled by bats. And for good reason. Even now, travelers grumble that their horses and pack animals become so exhausted by repeated bat attacks that they are unable to work. Just as aggravating, wounds from vampire bat bites on an animal's withers can preclude the use of a saddle for riding or a pack frame for carrying cargo.

Complaints involving cattle are even more vociferous. Although reports of cattle being so weakened by loss of blood as to be on the verge of death are rarely substantiated, many cows do suffer severely from vampire bat attacks. U.S. Fish and Wildlife Service biologists have conducted vampire bat control programs on ranches where cattle *averaged* around four fresh bites a night. These same biologists, working under R. Daniel Thompson, were also able to show that repeated loss of blood from vampire bats could inhibit the production of milk in dairy cows pastured in marginal grazing areas. Immature cattle especially suffer from vampire bat depredations, and claims have been made that cattle cannot gain weight in certain parts of South America due to the presence of these "blood-thirsty demons." The open wounds left by vampire bats are prone to infection and open to infestations by screw-worms and other insect pests. Scars left by feeding bats reduce the commercial value of hides and can disfigure show animals. The udders and teats of cows and pigs may even be so scarified as to prohibit their offspring from suckling.

Nor are smaller animals free of the vampire bat's visits. Numerous accounts stress the need for poultry to be housed at night in special pens under ground, beneath upturned canoes, or in clay pots to protect them from marauding bats. One traveler, L.M. Nesbitt, observing the results of vampire bats in Venezuela, noted that, "They even prey upon pigs and farmyard chickens: the former becoming in course of time like empty collapsed leather bags, and the latter like hollow bladders with a few feathers stuck in them at different angles." A more typical but less picturesque result is for vampire bats to kill chickens and other fowls during the night by extracting more blood than the birds can withstand.

Not even dogs escape the bats' attentions, especially in areas where livestock are wanting. Writing of a situation in Ecuador, Alfred Simson observed that one dog was so favored by vampire bats that it only recovered when placed under a large earthen pot at night. William Beebe and his wife Mary, inveterate reporters of vampire bat activities, stated that their servants had to collect the chair cushions on a veranda each evening and place them under upturned chairs. To not do so was to risk the dogs bleeding on the cushions while sleeping on them when the bats were about.

If blood losses alone are calculated, it is easy to become alarmed at the vampire bat's potential for mischief. Assuming that each bat ingests 20 ccs. of blood during its nightly visit, and that an equal amount is lost through protracted bleeding, the amount of blood drawn is just under 15 quarts a year. Just one colony of vampires would therefore draw about 365 gallons of the vital fluid -- the contents of 27 cows, 20 horses, 365 goats, or 4600 chickens! Should it be possible to arrive at the total number of vampire bats present in just one South or Central American country, the amount of blood withdrawn could truly be said to be of biblical proportions. Fortunately, such figures mean very little in themselves. Large mammals, unless in sub-optimum condition, quickly replace the amounts of blood normally lost to vampire bats -- even in areas where an animal might suffer an average of several bites a night.

Reliable figures are obviously difficult to obtain, but reasonable estimates of livestock losses to vampire bats have ranged from one half million to two million head a year, representing annual costs of between 50 million and a quarter billion dollars. Brazil, Mexico, and Colombia are particularly hard hit, these countries suffering several million dollars worth of damage a year to cattle alone. These losses, however, are not so much due to injury and loss of blood, but to fatal and debilitating diseases transmitted through the bat's bite.

VAMPIRE BATS AS RESERVOIRS OF DISEASE

> They say, that from the marshes of that river, there come certain bats in the night season as big as turtle doves, invading men and biting them with a deadly wound, as some of them testify which have been bitten by the same. I myself communicating with Ancifus the Lieutenant whom they respected, and among other things asking him of the venomous biting of these bats, he told me that he was bitten by one of them on the heel, his foot lying uncovered in the night by reason of the heat in summer season: But that it hurt him no more, than if he had been bitten by any other beast not venomous. Others say, that the biting of some of them is venomous: Yet that the same is healed incontinently, if it be washed with water of the sea.

> Pietro Martyre Anghiera, ca. 1510
> (Transcribed from an Old English
> translation of a Spanish letter by Richard
> Eden)

It is an unpleasant fact that vampire bats are "carriers" of at least one fatal human disease and two deadly livestock afflictions. The most important of these is rabies. According to reports collected by veterinary neurologist Danny Brass, rabies transmitted by vampire bats is known to have resulted in the deaths of several hundred people, as well as tens of thousands of cattle and other animals. Numerous other fatal cases of vampire bat-borne rabies have undoubtedly occurred, the deaths going either unnoticed, or attributed to "just another deadly tropical pestilence."

Rabies

He was far beyond any human aid, but he was suffering frightfully. His arms bore the teeth marks of hogs, just as did those awful bodies on the floor, except of course, that the dead had been unable to move against such a horror, while the raving man had. I could do nothing except inject morphine, which I did, at once. The convulsions ceased, the horrible snarling sounds from his throat diminished. Finally they died away entirely and he sank into a stupor. Then I sat back until he died.

Herbert Spencer Dickey, 1929, *The Misadventures of a Tropical Medico.*

Rabies has always been, and in part remains, a mysterious disease. Found in both the Old and New Worlds, this contagious malady has plagued man and his animals throughout history. The cause of the disease is a virus that attacks the central nervous system of mammals, and the usual means of transmission is through the saliva received in the bite of an infected carnivore. More unorthodox methods of infection include inhaling air-borne rabies virus in bat caves, butchering the meat of rabies infected livestock, and handling rabid animals. Each host has its own species-adapted strain of the virus, and the chances of infection are influenced by numerous factors including the strain involved, the severity and location of the bite, and the recipient's resistance. The incubation period, or the time it takes the virus to travel to the spinal cord and brain, may vary from several days to more than a year, but is usually about three weeks. This is the time when the disease first becomes apparent. Once a person or an animal exhibits clinical signs of infection, the disease is invariably fatal. Fortunately for those exposed to rabies, effective vaccines are now available provided that the inoculations are given prior to the onset of any symptoms of the disease.

Rabies has been found in a wide variety of bats including the three species of vampires. The common vampire bat, however, is an ideal vector for transmitting the disease. Not only does the animal

69

make its nightly living biting other mammals, its life history facilitates the spread of rabies among its fellows. Spending their day in a warm, humid cavern, infected vampire bats can pass on virus-containing saliva when grooming their roostmates, when regurgitating food to other members of the colony, and most importantly, through males biting other bats in their many squabbles and rivalries. No wonder then that when rabid insect-eating bats began showing up in the United States in the 1950s, some people assumed that these bats had contracted the virus from rabid vampire bats while wintering in the tropics. This does not appear to be the case, however, as studies of the strains of virus found in insectivorous bats shows them to be different from those found in vampire bats.

It appears that vampire bats have had a long history with rabies, and are relatively resistant to the virus. But just how members of a vampire colony initially contract rabies is uncertain. They do not become infected by feeding on rabid animals, as the virus is not present in sufficient quantities in the blood to be infectious. Scientists formerly thought that some vampire bats became "carriers," that is, they were exposed to a less than lethal dose of the virus, recovered, and then went on to transmit the virus to more susceptible bats. Recent research has shown that only those vampire bats that eventually show signs of the disease and die are able to transmit rabies to laboratory animals. No bat that remained healthy has ever been known to transmit rabies to an uninfected animal.

Even though the usual incubation period is from two to four weeks, after which time the bat's saliva usually contains the rabies virus, vampire bats have infected laboratory animals for up to four months before showing any signs of rabies. "Sick" bats may become irritable and display such erratic behavior as flying about during the daytime. Symptoms vary, however, and an infected bat may quietly succumb of the "dumb" or paralytic form of the disease, or go through a "furious" phase in which the bat aggressively attacks other animals. In either case, once stricken, the bat dies within a few days.

Any mammal, including man, can become infected by the bite of a rabid vampire bat, but the usual victims are other vampire bats and cattle. Bovine rabies is a pervasive and devastating disease throughout much of Latin America where it is variously known as *derrengue* (from the Spanish verb *derrengar* meaning to severely injure the back), *el tronchado* (the broken down-one), or *mal de cadera* (hip sickness). It is not uncommon for bovine rabies to kill from 20 to 50 percent of the cattle in a given area, and the disease can spell economic ruin for large and small ranchers alike. Unfortunately, a natural response is for the rancher to immediately send any cattle showing signs of the disease to market in an attempt to minimize his loss. While such a strategy poses little danger to the consumer, there is some risk in butchering sick

70

animals. In one survey of a Mexico City slaughterhouse, forty out of a thousand randomly checked cattle tested positive for rabies!

Only after the incubation period of several weeks has passed does an infected animal show any signs of rabies. Even then, the early stages of the disease are not always readily apparent to an inexperienced observer and can be mistaken for a variety of other ailments. In livestock, there is an initial period of restlessness or excitement, often accompanied by a grinding of the teeth. An increasing paralysis of the hindquarters is soon observed as the animal trembles and staggers about. Shortly thereafter the animal lies down and cannot get up. In her continuing efforts to do so, a cow may dig a circular pit around herself with her front feet. The animal now refuses to eat or drink and becomes constipated. Salivation is heavy as the cow cannot swallow. Eventually the paralysis moves forward to the front legs, the animal becomes emaciated, and in three to five days, dies of respiratory failure and other complications.

Incidences of humans contracting rabies from vampire bats are relatively rare, averaging only about ten reported cases a year. Should someone be so unfortunate as to contract rabies from a vampire bat, the symptoms are usually, but not always, of the paralytic form of the disease. Like bovine rabies, the first symptoms are typical of any number of illnesses -- a general feeling of malaise, headache, and sometimes a slight fever. A tingling or numbness may also be felt in the vicinity of the bite. Usually within four days or so after the onset of these symptoms paralysis sets in, and the patient may suffer from tremors, constipation, or incontinence. Often there is a strong aversion to drinking water and any attempt to take fluids brings on a convulsive reaction (hence the disease's common name of hydrophobia). Swallowing is impossible and the patient becomes disoriented and apprehensive. As the disease develops, the senses may become impaired, and the paralysis spreads throughout the body. In some cases the victim behaves irrationally and even attacks those around him. Death usually occurs from respiratory or cardiac failure in about two weeks, although some patients have survived on modern life support systems for close to a month. The symptoms of rabies are so agonizing, and the death so horrible, that medical personnel who have observed the symptoms of the disease in themselves have committed suicide rather than face the horror that they knew was coming.

History of Vampire Bat-borne Rabies: Rabies in vampire bats is nothing new. Accounts of conquistadors and other early travelers described animals and men dying after being bitten by vampire bats in Panama, Mexico, and Guatemala. At least two towns in the Mexican state of Chiapas were reported to have been abandoned during colonial times due to losses suffered from vampire bats. In 1745, after a visit to Ecuador, La Condimine reported that "blood-sucking bats" had destroyed "all the great cattle introduced there by the missionaries." Alfred Wallace was told in 1848 that many cattle had been killed by vampire bats on an island at the mouth of the Amazon. Gaston de Verteuil, in his history of Trinidad, described an 1856 epidemic of what was obviously bovine rabies. But because no mad dogs or other rabid animals were in evidence, and because no one then suspected bats of transmitting rabies, the cause of these deaths was unknown.

Bovine rabies was first recognized as a serious problem in the early 1900s when an epidemic began killing livestock in southern Brazil. Before the epidemic had run its course, more than 4000 head of cattle and over 1000 horses had died. A number of these animals had been diagnosed as rabies positive in the laboratory, but how they got the disease remained a mystery. Mad dogs were still assumed to be the source of infection even though no rabid dogs were found biting cattle, and bats had been observed attacking cattle in bright sunlight. It was not until 1916, when a fruit bat was diagnosed as being rabid, that bats were shown to be able to transmit the rabies virus. Further studies followed, and by the early 1920s, rabid vampire bats were strongly suspected as having been the cause of Brazil's "cattle plague."

The vampire bat's role as a transmitter of rabies was nonetheless still not generally appreciated. When cattle began dying of an unknown malady on the island of Trinidad in 1923, their deaths were attributed to the animals having eaten oleander leaves. Two years later another major outbreak of this "new" cattle disease struck the island. The Director of Agriculture attributed the cause of these deaths to botulism, a position he maintained throughout a similar epidemic in 1928. Even when a 15-year-old boy succumbed to what was diagnosed as a form of rabies in 1929, the original diagnosis was rejected in favor of polio. Only after another dozen people were dead, and laboratory tests conclusively showed that they died of rabies, was the seriousness of the problem realized. But how these people and cattle acquired rabies remained an enigma. The island was free of rabid dogs and none of the people infected had reported being bitten by a vampire bat or any other animal. Only after the deaths of several more individuals and numerous experiments were government pathologist Dr. J.L. Pawan and his colleagues able to prove that both the livestock and human deaths were due to paralytic rabies, and that the virus was being transmitted by vampire bats.

During the next 20 years, outbreaks of vampire bat-borne rabies were reported in both people and livestock in Mexico, Honduras, and British Guiana. The disease has since been reported in every country in which vampire bats occur except Chile. The most recent outbreak of vampire bat transmitted rabies has been in Peru's Amazon Basin where the virus has killed countless numbers of livestock. In two nearby rural communities, no fewer than 29 people had succumbed to vampire bat-borne rabies during the first four months of 1990 alone.

Epizootics: For reasons not fully understood, cases of vampire bat-borne rabies tend to occur in periodic outbreaks, or as they are called in the medical profession, *epizootics*. After a period of from several weeks to several months, the epizootic typically dies out, only to break out again in another vicinity. These epizootics thus move in waves through the countryside, generally at a rate of about 25 to 40 miles-per-year. The size and width of the area affected by the epizootic may vary, but the front of the wave is usually from two to ten miles wide depending on the terrain and cover. Once an epizootic in a particular area wanes, four or more years usually elapse before another occurs.

The progress of an epizootic can be determined by the immune response of the bats. In areas where a rabies outbreak is in progress, a significant percentage of the vampire bats present will test positive for the rabies virus, and few if any of the bats will have rabies antibodies in their serum. Conversely, in areas where an epidemic is receding, antibody levels in vampire bats are high, and no evidence of the virus is detected. In uninfected areas, the bats possess neither the rabies virus nor its antibodies.

Just as summer "dog days" are associated with cases of canine rabies, outbreaks of vampire bat-borne rabies also tend to be seasonal. Epizootics on Trinidad and in much of South America have been definitely linked to the summer rainy season; outbreaks in Mexico occur most often during the winter months. Rexford Lord, after studying rabies outbreaks throughout South America, hypothesized that these episodes are the result of a synchronization in vampire bat births. He believes that epizootics are the result of large numbers of newly weaned bats going forth and setting up territories in areas where vampire bats have previously been exposed to the virus. The young bats, having no rabies antibodies, are highly susceptible to the disease and quickly become infected. Others maintain that the seasonal nature of the outbreaks is due to changes in livestock availability. *Quien sabe?*

Other Diseases Transmitted by Vampire Bats

Obviously the vampires had returned in force, for [my horse] was not the only sufferer. Four of the mules had dried runnels of blood plastered over their bodies, but Bee-Mason's animal almost made us cry. Its haunches had fallen in, it dragged its feet as if it were numb, and a pair of dull eyes looked from the bottom of what appeared to be wells.

73

Clearly, it was dying, and we hastened its end with a merciful shot.

Julian Duguid, 1931, *Green Hell*

Murrina: (malaise), also known as Panama horse disease, surra, and *mal de caderas* (hip illness), is a blood disease of horses, mules and donkeys which was introduced to the New World tropics from the Old World in the 16th and 17th centuries. The infective agents are protozoans that are spread from animal to animal by blood-sucking horse flies and vampire bats. Although cattle are symptomless reservoirs of the disease, infected horses and dogs experience fever, difficulty in breathing, loss of appetite, and a weakness in the hind legs. Stricken animals become emaciated and many of the horses eventually die.

Because of the large quantities of blood consumed, vampire bats are potent vectors of *murrina*. Vampire bats can even transmit this disease to horses from infected cattle, something horse flies cannot do as too few protozoans are usually present in the cow's blood for the flies to transmit an infection. Infected bats may die or recover, those that survive acting as *murrina* reservoirs for several months. The number of horses lost from this disease, while locally significant, is difficult to ascertain. Some of the clinical symptoms of *murrina* are similar to other diseases (including bovine rabies), and many cases go unreported.

Venezuelan Equine Encephalomyelitis: Like rabies, VEE is caused by a virus that attacks the nervous system. Normally carried from host to host by mosquitos, this disease has been shown to be naturally present in vampire bats in Mexico, Guatemala, and Ecuador. Infected bats show no signs of illness, but symptoms in humans and horses include a high fever that may be lethal. Although people rarely succumb from the disease, approximately half of the infected horses die. As with paralytic rabies, however, preventative vaccines are available.

Potential Diseases: Vampire bats, because of their feeding habits, are potential transmitters of a variety of other tropical diseases affecting man and his livestock. Hypothetically, these include the dreaded yellow fever or *vomito*, foot and mouth disease, hepatitis, brucellosis, Chagas disease (commonly transmitted by blood-sucking bugs), and even malaria. Should the HIV virus that causes AIDS (acquired immune-deficiency syndrome) be shown to be transmitted by vampire bats, the bat's nightmarish reputation would be fulfilled indeed.

VAMPIRE BAT CONTROL

> The vampire bat is a nuisance to human beings and
> animals alike, and a fortune awaits the enterprising person
> who commercializes the use of its fur.
>
> Colonel Percy Hamilton Fawcett, *Lost
> Trails, Lost Cities*, 1953

Native Americans had of necessity been co-existing with
vampire bats for thousands of years, and European immigrants quickly
adopted some of the local wisdom for coping with these pests. The
Guajira Indians of northern South America sewed a lace-like skirt on to
their hammocks, in what, was in essence, the precursor of the mosquito
net. Other Indians sought protection by wrapping themselves in their
hammocks at night or by sleeping with their heads and bodies enveloped
inside a blanket. Smokey fires of red peppers and other astringents
were also kept burning throughout the night to keep these marauders at
bay -- precautions which were not only less than totally successful but
which came at a great expense in comfort. Ducks, turkeys, and other
domestic fowls were kept at night in bat-proof enclosures. Less
demanding, but of more questionable value, was the use of "bat-banes,"
various aromatic herbs hung in houses and around one's neck. One of
these plants, *sabilla*, has been used as a vampire bat repellent in
Venezuela into recent times. If a person was bitten by a vampire bat, a
standard remedy was to cauterize the wound with a hot coal and rub in
ashes to staunch the bleeding.

The importation of large domestic animals presented additional
problems that would increase in time as vampire bat populations
adapted to this serendipitous new food supply. In their attempts to
thwart the growing scourge of "blood-letting bats," the settlers
surrounded their corrals and dwellings with barricades of thorny
bushes. Various "preventatives" were also applied to the backs of
horses or rubbed into old wounds as a means of warding off attacks.
Some of the concoctions recommended included ground red peppers;
tobacco mixed with salt and soot; an ointment made of camphor, soap,
and petroleum; jaguar grease; and, in what must have had its origin in
Old World vampyrology, garlic. Cattle, except for the family milk cow
which might be kept in a barn, were especially difficult to protect, and
often had to be left to fend for themselves on the open range. This
prompted some rather unorthodox attempts to reduce the number of
vampire bat attacks. Ranchers in Venezuela even imported domestic
pigeons in the belief that these birds drive vampire bats away or provide
them with an alternate food source.

Required equipment for a traveler in "vampire country" at the turn of the 20th century included a mosquito net and a kerosene lantern. It had been found that a light kept burning throughout the night, while not infallible, was the best means of keeping the bats at bay, both from one's own person and from his mount. A heavy jute sleeping bag or better yet, a tent that could be entirely closed, was also deemed advisable, even though the heat inside might be oppressive almost beyond endurance. Although wire screening was a Godsend for residents, travelers still had to make some inconvenient adjustments in order to protect themselves and their animals. L.M. Nesbitt described the patio of an inn in a vampire-infested area of Venezuela he visited in 1936. Not only was the patio covered over with a rope net to keep vampire bats out, the horse stalls were "huge cages made of wire netting, or in some instances, the sides were made of reeds and the top only of wire netting. In these cages, mules, horses, and donkeys were kept at night. Even some of the people themselves, such of them as did not possess mosquito-nets, slept inside the wire cages so as to be protected from the scourge."

Figure 32. Vampire bat entangled in a mist net. Vampire bats appear to "fight the net" more vigorously than most other species of bats. Photo by author.

With the knowledge in the 1930s that vampire bats were the primary transmitters of bovine rabies in the American tropics, the prevention of bat bites took on a special urgency. This was especially so on the island of Trinidad where bat-borne rabies was killing not only animals but humans. Scientists were therefore dispatched to the island from Europe and the United States with the mission of reducing the population of vampire bats. Eventually, it was hoped, a way could be found to rid the island of bats entirely. To this end, a variety of traps, snares, and nets were employed, the most promising being the mist net, a woven lattice of silk or other fine fiber, that had long been used to capture birds in the Orient. But, while some vampire bats were caught in mist nets placed around dwellings and pastures, the numbers of bats that could be killed in this fashion were too few to reduce the incidences of bites on the island. A more promising technique was for a worker to take advantage of the bats' penchant for visiting previous wounds and apply a strychnine paste, sweetened with a drop of sugar syrup, on the fresh bite of a cow. Vampire bats alighted on the treated area, licked the wound, and died in seconds. This technique, too, had its limits, as the paste could only be applied to areas where the cow or other animal could not lick the poison and endanger itself. More importantly, applying the strychnine required too much time and labor to be practical for treating large herds of range cattle.

It soon became apparent that the only way to destroy large numbers of vampire bats was to attack them in their roosts. Caves and hollow silk-cotton trees were sought out and any bats inside driven out with dense fumes of burning sulphur and dispatched with shotguns. Roosts were also treated with poisonous cyanide dust. Where poisoning or smoking the bats out was impractical, the caves and tree cavities were sealed with netting and the bats inside either captured with hand nets or shot in the roosts. Bounties of up to $20 per vampire bat were paid, and special "bat boys" were hired to locate roosts and destroy what were soon regarded as "very smart bats." These activities intensified in 1941 when the U.S. military built a 20 square mile base on Trinidad and put Captain Lloyd Rolland Gates in charge of mosquito and vampire bat control. Gates not only kept five "bat boys" constantly busy, military personnel cleared caves of roosting bats by using flamethrowers, poison gas, and dynamite. Still, the vampire bats persisted. There were just too many roosts and hiding places to find them all.

Additional rabies outbreaks, not only on Trinidad, but in other countries, triggered a near vampire bat hysteria after World War II. During a series of rabies epidemics in Mexico, during which a farmer and his three children died after being bitten by a rabid bat in Sinaloa, teams of specialists incinerated tens of thousands of bats with flamethrowers. Literally thousands of caves in South America were also pumped full of poison gas and dynamited at great risk to the workers. Panama's spectacular Caves of Chilibrillo were demolished, and in Brazil, a cavern was installed with an elaborate network of wires designed to electrocute vampire bats. By the 1960s, Venezuela was claiming to be destroying a million bats a year through the use of similar methods. Perhaps the most ill-considered operation, however, took place in Colombia where a virulent strain of Newcastle's virus was aerosolized into a cave. The idea was to infect vampire bats so that they would carry and spread this deadly disease to other bat populations, as myxomatosis had been used to kill rabbits in Australia. Although the Newcastle virus was said to have killed about 5000 bats, including some vampires, such measures posed a serious long-term danger to other species of wildlife, not to mention people and domestic animals.

Despite these efforts, and the destruction of countless numbers of harmless and beneficial bats, vampire bats and bat-borne rabies continued to be a serious problem. If anything, common vampire bats increased as new ranches were carved out of tropical forests. When an intensive survey in 1966 concluded that half a million cattle a year were dying of rabies, the World Health Organization declared vampire bats to be the most important wildlife disease vector in Latin America. Yet, in 1967, when the Brazilian government asked Bernardo Villa, Mexico's premier bat biologist, for his recommendations, he had to advise them that, "No notable success has been achieved in controlling...*Desmodus rotundus* in any of the countries of tropical America."

Even the veterinary profession seemed unable to offer any relief. Although immunizing vaccines had been available for both livestock and humans since the 1930s, and several countries had initiated inoculation programs, the results so far had been disappointing. Vaccines had to be imported to the stricken area and required special care and handling to insure effectiveness. Injections could cost as much as a $100 per cow, and even when given, were often administered too late to do any good. Reported failure rates were high. Moreover, preventative vaccines could neither reduce the number of vampire bat bites, nor be given to all of the rural people who might be exposed to vampire bat borne rabies.

The 1960s was a time when Yankee "know-how" was touted as being the answer to the economic ills plaguing "developing" nations. Given the ineffective and destructive nature of vampire bat control programs south of the border, and the belief that vampire bats might one day invade the southern United States, a number of organizations including the U.S. Agency for International Development (AID), the Pan American Health Organization (PAHO), and the United Nation's Food and Agricultural Organization (FAO) began conducting vampire bat research. Together, and separately, these agencies set out to devise an effective method of vampire bat control. What no one then realized was that in this effort at least, the results would exceed almost everyone's expectations.

In 1967, AID requested the Fish and Wildlife Service, the agency then responsible for predator and rodent control in the United States, for assistance in combating vampire bats. Having recently developed the potent predacide Compound 1080, and eliminated the wolf from the western U.S. and northern Mexico, the agency was a logical choice. However, the assignment was not an easy one. Times were changing and environmental considerations were now of greater concern. The Service's mission was to devise a vampire bat control technique that was not only safe and effective for use by rural people, but one that was selective only for vampire bats, and that posed no danger to the environment. The program was to proceed on two fronts: conduct studies into the vampire bat's natural history to determine when the animal was most vulnerable, and develop a suitable vampiricide through laboratory experiments at the Service's Denver Wildlife Research Center.

After two years of study, researcher S. B. Linhart came up with a highly ingenious concept. Laboratory experiments had shown that vampire bats were highly susceptible to anticoagulants used to kill rodents. When ingested, anticoagulants block the clotting action of blood, weaken the blood vessels, and cause uncontrolled bleeding. Vampire bats fed even a minute amount of an anticoagulant quickly died of massive internal hemorrhaging. Linhart, who had observed vampire bats grooming each other, now decided to apply an anticoagulant paste to a captive vampire bat and allow the bat to return to its colony. Within two weeks, the test animal and 18 of its 20 roost-mates were dead. Ironically, an anticoagulant, one of the vampire bat's most specialized adaptations for survival, was also the key to its destruction.

This technique, which came to be known as the *topical method*, was then field tested on two ranches in Mexico. Taking advantage of the bats' habit of feeding during moonless portions of the night, American and Mexican workers captured vampire bats in mist nets placed around cattle held in corrals. Netted vampire bats were kept in holding cages until midnight, when an estimated 75 percent of the feeding bats had been caught, and smeared with a mixture of vaseline and either of two brands of anticoagulants. Follow-up studies showed that the colonies to which the vampire bats belonged were substantially reduced within a week to 10 days, and that from 20 to 40 vampire bats were killed for each bat treated. Ninety percent of the bats visiting the corrals were destroyed in one night's work, and after a second treatment a month later, the number of cattle being bitten was reduced to zero. Later tests were equally impressive, the number of bites being reduced in every case between 94 and 97%. Because of the vampire bat's low reproductive rate, these treatments measurably lowered the incidence of vampire bat depredations for periods of from three to five years.

Figure 33. Captured vampire bats are smeared with an anticoagulant mixed with vaseline and released. The anticoagulant is then ingested through grooming by not only the treated animal, but by other members of the colony to which it belongs. From 20 to 40 bats will thus die of internal hemorrhaging for each vampire captured.

A variation of the topical method was to smear an anticoagulant mixture directly on the walls of caves and other roost sites used by vampire bats. Besides being effective, this modification had the distinct advantage of workers not having to handle possibly rabid bats. Its principal drawbacks were that the bats' daytime retreats had to be located, and the danger the technique posed to non-target bats using the same roost sites. To prevent killing other species of bats, great care must be taken to apply the anticoagulant mixture to only those areas where vampire bat droppings predominate.

At the same time as the topical method was being developed, R.D. Thompson at the Denver Wildlife Research Center was taking another approach. After injecting cattle with small quantities of various insecticides in an unsuccessful attempt to kill feeding vampire bats, Thompson hit on the idea of injecting a minute suspension of an anticoagulant into the rumen of a cow. What he found out was that the anticoagulant circulated in the cow's blood for three days, killing any vampire bat that fed on the animal. Later, tests on three ranches in Mexico showed that the number of bat bites on treated cattle declined by more than 90% within two weeks. There were several problems with this *systemic method*, however. Besides being limited to ruminant animals, intraruminal injections require expertise in veterinary medicine and the animal's milk and meat are unfit for human consumption while the anticoagulant is circulating in the cow's blood. This latter aspect was particularly worrisome to the U.S. government in that it not only shared responsibility for the technique's development, large quantities of Central and South American beef were being exported to America by fast-food hamburger chains. Another detriment was that the anticoagulant could be fatal if injected into calves under a year old as the insufficiently developed rumen in young animals is not yet capable of producing vitamin K which stimulates blood to clot. There was also the expense of rounding up the cattle prior to treatment.

Figure 34. Injecting a cow with an anticoagulant. U.S. Fish and Wildlife Service photo courtesy of Clay Mitchell.

Nonetheless, both anticoagulant methods promised to be effective tools in combating vampire bat-borne rabies, especially if conducted in conjunction with the World Health Organization's ongoing effort to coordinate and expand cattle immunization programs in Latin America. Accordingly, Clay Mitchell and other American advisors launched a massive training and demonstration program. Between 1974 and 1978, anti-vampire bat campaigns were initiated throughout the bat's range. The results were impressive -- especially in arid regions where cattle tend to be concentrated around water. Rumen injections reduced the number of vampire bat bites in every area treated by at least 80 percent. Bat bites in problem areas in Brazil and Ecuador declined 99 percent. Reductions in bat bites were not the only benefit. R.D. Thompson and his cooperators showed that milk production significantly increased on at least one ranch in Nicaragua after treatment. What was especially impressive, cost analyses demonstrated that 100 cattle could be treated for only $15, or 15 cents a head.

In the late 1970s, Raul Flores-Crespo, in conjunction with a team of researchers with the Pan American Health Organization in Mexico, improved on the systemic method. Using this technique, a small amount of anticoagulant solution, aptly named Vampirinip III, is injected directly into an animal's muscle tissue where it circulates in the blood for several days. While in the cow's blood the anticoagulant is lethal to vampire bats for up to four days as opposed to three days for intraruminal injections. Field tests in Yucatán and San Luis Potosí showed this method to be nearly as effective as the topical and earlier systemic methods, bat bites declining between 75 and 90 percent within two weeks of treatment. Some of the advantages of intramuscular injections are that they can be given to horses and calves as well as to cattle, and can be administered by ranchmen without any veterinary training. Most importantly, workers do not need to be able to identify the species of bat or handle potentially rabid animals. Nor do they need to find the bats' roost sites.

Any of these techniques can be successfully used to block the progress of a rabies outbreak. The control procedure recommended by vampire control expert Rexford Lord is to plot the occurence of reported rabies cases and determine the direction in which the epidemic appears to be moving. The path of the epidemic will usually follow defined ecological avenues of vampire bat habitat along a river or corridors of tropical forest. Areas to be treated may therefore vary in size from less than a half of a square mile to as large as 30 square miles. Control stations should then be established about two miles apart within the corridors, each treatment area covering approximately 10 square miles of habitat. The important thing is to treat areas in advance of the epizootic's direction of movement.

Regardless of which anticoagulant method is used, five consecutive nights of treatment usually suffice to halt the epizootic's progress. A prompt response is of course essential, and a common, though understandable mistake, is to focus treatment on those ranches where livestock are dying. These cattle are already beyond help. Vampire bat numbers in these areas are already declining, and the epidemic has moved on to new pastures.

The benefits of these new anticoagulant methods were amply illustrated by a different method of control in the Argentine's Gran

Chaco region. In an attempt to thwart an advancing rabies epizootic, in the 1970s, cyanide gas was pumped into scores of underground wells which provided the primary roost sites for vampire bats in this arid area. Although the vampire bat population was depleted as a result, and the progress of the rabies outbreak halted, the cost was high. The project leader was killed when his gasmask failed while he was inspecting a well, causing him to lose consciousness and fall to his death.

An even newer development is an oral vaccine that immunizes the vampire bats themselves against rabies. In this method, a vaccine containing mixture is applied to the backs of from two to five percent of the cattle in the path of a rabies epidemic. Bats feeding on treated animals come in contact with the mixture which is then ingested along with the vaccine by the bat and its roost-mates during communal grooming. This procedure, which is still in the experimental stages, has the promise of being the best means of bovine rabies control yet as colonies of immunized bats cannot sustain an epizootic. And, even though this immunization method would not alleviate the damage done by bat bites, it would significantly lessen the danger of humans contracting rabies from vampire bats.

The total control of vampire bat-borne rabies is impossible. Even with an army of specialists, and the participation of every rancher in tropical America, reservoirs of rabid vampire bats would still persist deep within tropical rainforests and in other refugia. But thanks to the use of these anticoagulant methods in conjunction with increasingly efficient livestock immunization programs, the number of cases of bovine rabies is now on the wane. And, with the cost of control constantly being reduced, there is reason to expect this trend to continue. Modern control methods, besides being safe and effective, can now arrest vampire bat-borne rabies outbreaks without harming other forms of wildlife or exterminating the vampire bat as a species. To completely eliminate such a fascinating creature would be an irrevocable tragedy.

Prevention and First Aid for Humans: Hunters, nature photographers, prospectors, anyone spending the night out-of-doors in vampire bat habitat, should be aware of the possibility of being bitten. Camping equipment should include a closeable tent, mosquito netting, and a lantern. Spelunkers exploring caves and biologists handling bats are considered to be at a higher than average risk of contracting bat-borne rabies and need to take additional precautions. Heavy leather gloves are essential apparel for biologists handling bats. It is also strongly suggested that people working with bats obtain a regimen of pre-exposure rabies shots even though they are expensive and not without the possibility of side-effects. Anti-rabies injections are especially prudent if one plans to be in a remote region far from modern medical facilities. These shots, usually two or three in number and given intramuscularly over a three day period, can be obtained from a physician or at a health clinic for about $350. Needless to say, the quality and potency of the serum needs to be of the highest standard.

Should you be bitten by a bat, wash the wound immediately with soap and water before applying a disinfectant. Because rabies is a fatal disease, all bat bites must be considered potentially hazardous. If possible, capture or kill the bat, taking care not to damage the head, so that it can be checked for rabies in a laboratory. Although it may be desirable to refrigerate the head, do not freeze it. If the bat is not available, or if several days have elapsed since the bite was received, you will want to go as soon as possible to a health clinic or a physician and begin a series of post-exposure antirabies inoculations. The Center for Disease Control recommends that Americans get these in the U.S. if possible to reduce the possibility of an allergic reaction to the animal cultivated serums used in many countries. After receiving an initial Rabies Immune Globulin shot, you will be given four additional antirabies vaccine inoculations after intervals of three, seven, fourteen, and twenty-eight days. These shots should be given in the muscle of the upper arm and not in the buttocks. The old standard "Pasteur treatment" of injecting a vaccine into the abdomen is no longer given, and I can personally attest that the treatment now is no more painful than any other immunization.

VAMPIRE BATS IN CAPTIVITY

Although Vamp served her purpose as an object of study, she did not help Roderick to pay the expenses of his trip. In two weeks she began to languish, and in three weeks he freed her rather than see her die. The world's zoos are still in the market for a live and thriving vampire bat, seemingly impossible to keep captive.

Willard Price, "The Mystery of the Vampire Bat," 1950

In actuality, the common vampire bat does very well in captivity. Rugged and adaptable, this bat displays neither stress nor panic when placed in a cage, and tolerates a wide range of temperatures if the humidity is sufficient and adequate amounts of fresh blood are supplied. While naturally suspicious and aggressive, vampire bats readily accommodate to human activity. Most captives become relatively tame within a few days, behave like pets, and even refrain from biting their handler.

Vampire bats were first kept as laboratory study animals in the early 1930s in their native Brazil, Panama, and Trinidad. Here it was learned that they could be fed cow blood, provided that it was first whipped with a bundle of straws, or stirred with a mass of glass beads, to remove the fibrin which causes blood to clot. This defibrinated blood, looking like bright red wine, proved to be ideal for feeding vampire bats as it does not clot and can be stored in a refrigerator.

Armed with this knowledge, Raymond Ditmars and Arthur Greenhall captured a vampire bat in Panama in 1933 and successfully transported it to the Reptile House at the New York Zoological Park for exhibition. This bat, a female, lived for several months, and even produced a pup during her confinement. Both mother and offspring proved enormously popular with the public and made the newspapers from "coast to coast." A second expedition in 1935, this time to the island of Trinidad, resulted in four more vampire bats being shipped to the New York Zoological Park where they survived for up to six years. Since then vampire bats have been exhibited at numerous institutions throughout the world. Other colonies have been maintained in research laboratories from New York state to Argentina, as well as in England and Germany. Some of these populations have been self-sustaining for many years, and at least one vampire bat has lived in captivity for nearly 20 years.

Depending on the number of bats to be housed, the vampire bat's quarters may be anywhere from as small as a one-square-foot cage for a laboratory animal to the size of an average living room for a colony on display to the public. The bat's surroundings must be well ventilated, and the humidity should be kept above 60% -- 100% is not too high. Temperatures should range between 75 and 78 degrees F., and not drop much below 70 degrees or rise above 82 degrees. Captive vampire bats can, and will, adjust themselves to increasing amounts of light and a conditioned bat will function nicely in either a dimly lighted exhibit, or in an environment having regular periods of daylight and darkness. Vampire bats prefer to feed on the ground and hang from the roof or top of their cage, so that confinements simulating natural caverns are ideal.

Defibrinated cattle or pig blood obtained from a butcher shop and kept in a refrigerator is the captive vampire bat's usual fare. Vampire bats at the Houston zoo fed outdated human plasma from blood banks did not do as well as animals fed fresh cattle blood, and the Houston colony failed to maintain itself on this diet. Frozen cow blood is said to be acceptable to vampire bats, but it must be used within 10 to 12 hours after thawing as it soon spoils. Vampire bats have no natural aversion to spoiled blood, and can get sick and die if their food becomes contaminated. Dried or "instant" blood, reconstituted with water, is best used only in emergencies.

After a day or two, the bats will readily take blood from a shallow dish, a drinking tube, or even a live animal. A gravity-fed drinking bottle, such as those used on rabbit farms, is best for multiple captives as it prevents any messes made by bats competing for food and splashing blood. As the animals become increasingly tame, they will forgo the usual pandemonium made on being disturbed, and eventually feed in semidarkness.

Most caretakers feed their animals just at dusk, allowing about 20 ccs. of blood per bat. If more than one vampire bat is present, the keeper should allow from 15 to 20 minutes for each animal to complete its meal. It is important to feed the bats regularly each night although an occasionally skipped meal does them no real harm. Caged vampire bats have fewer physical demands than their wild brethren, and even though they may appear much emaciated, captive animals can survive for up to three days without eating. Water and vitamin supplements are usually deemed unnecessary, although a dish of water or saline solution helps raise the humidity and forestalls critical dehydration should blood meals be temporarily unavailable. Vampire bats cannot be fed hamburger or other solid foods.

Should a breeding colony be desired, fifteen to 20 animals is a manageable group. The cage must be of sufficient size (five feet square or more) to prevent overcrowding and allow maturing males to withdraw into bachelor groups. Although females can be introduced into the colony at any time, adding a new male results in a fight. Pups, especially those in small cages, or those belonging to inexperienced mothers, are sometimes attacked by males, and it may be necessary to separate new mothers from the rest of the colony. Some youngsters also experience difficulty weaning at four to five months of age, and it may be necessary to hand-rear them with an eye-dropper. And, while adults never lose their power of flight, a young bat must be taught to fly, an impossibility in a small cage.

Keeping vampire bats presents some problems. The excrement, besides being copious, smelling bad, and being just downright nasty, is highly corrosive. Keeping cages or exhibits clean can therefore be difficult, and William Wimsatt and Anthony Guerriere designed a cage that minimized these problems. They recommended that the cage be of non-corrosive aluminum, and that the bottom be lined with damp paper towels to facilitate cleaning and to increase the humidity. The towels are replaced daily at which time the feeding utensils are also cleaned. Some innovative methods employed by zoos to sanitize their vampire bat displays have included lining the bottoms of exhibits with peat moss, and introducing giant cockroaches and other natural scavengers to assist in cleaning up the droppings.

The claws on the hind feet of vampire bats kept in small cages require trimming from time to time. Other than that, captive animals require little care other than feeding and cleaning their cells. Parasites, so common in wild vampire bats, apparently do not do well in artificial environments, and any present on captured animals soon disappear. Diseases among captive vampire bats are also rarely reported. Should one wish to study individual animals, the bats can be tagged on the forearm with an aluminum band or distinguished with punch marks on the wing. If one wishes to handle a vampire bat for any length of time, the bat can be sedated with chloroform.

Even though a captive may have become habituated to human contact, the danger of being bitten is of course always present. Escape is also a potential problem as the bats retain their natural agility, and are adept at hiding in nooks and crannies. Unlike other bats, escaped vampires do not startle or panic when they are discovered, and many a researcher has had a real hunt on his hands trying to recover a fugitive hiding in a laboratory.

While making exotic "pets," the maintenance of captive vampire bats is strongly discouraged for all but the most serious institutional studies. Legal restrictions aside, the care of captives is costly and constant and the vampire bat has little to recommend it as a pet. Nor, with the advent of quality nature programs on television, is there as much demand for the display of vampire bats. Like many other institutions, the Arizona-Sonora Desert Museum and Phoenix Zoo in my home state of Arizona discontinued their vampire bat exhibits years ago. Besides the danger of captive animals having rabies, there is always the chance for escapees and the establishment of an introduced population of vampire bats in Florida or south Texas. With rare exceptions, vampire bats are best left in their native habitats.

VAMPIRE BATS IN INDIAN MYTHOLOGY

If explorer's accounts are to be believed, hunting and food gathering peoples in Central and South America accepted vampire bats as just another blood-letting pest that they encountered on an almost daily, or more precisely, nocturnal basis. Nor did they consider these bats as especially dangerous or debilitating. Hence, vampire bats do not play an inordinate role in Indian legends and mythology when compared to more impressive animals such as the crocodile, tapir, and the jaguar. One of the few Indian legends involving vampire bats recorded by Europeans is a story related to ethnologist Walter Roth by the Arawak Indians of Guyana. In this saga, which describes a traditional journey to a distant land where there were stones ideal for making axes, the travelers are beset upon by vampire bats, that, like many legendary Arawak animals, are larger than life:

...Now this was in the country of the Bat Tribe, and the old man warned his crew that it was very dangerous for them to sling their hammocks on the trees because the Bats here were as large as cranes. He therefore called on them to build an inclosed camp, that is, a banab with covered sides. One young man, however, was slothful, and very backward in assisting the others to build the shelter. He said he did not believe that the Bats, however big they were, would hurt him before the morning. In spite of the old man's entreaties, he refused to come into the inclosure, but, fixing his hammock between two trees, rested outside. The others did as they were told, slinging their hammocks inside the banab. Late in the night, when it was quite dark, they heard the man outside entreating to be allowed to come in. But they said: "No. We cannot open the door now. You must bear what comes on you." And when they opened the door in the morning, all that was left of the individual was some bones. The Bats had sucked him dry indeed.

Figure 35. Mural by R. Auguiano depicting vampire bats in the Maya creation myth from the Popul Vuh. Photographed by the author at the National Museum of Anthropology in Mexico City.

Another Arawak legend repeated by Roth was that the owl was once married to the vampire bat's sister. The *vampira's* brothers would often accompany the owl and his mate on raids to people's houses, the owl first frightening the owners away with his eerie cry. Once, when the owl was away on other business, the bats went raiding without him. But not having the owl's call, they failed to frighten the people, and the village headman shot and stunned one of them with a blunt arrow. The next night the bats returned, and the same bat was again hit by an arrow, this time fatally. In retaliation, the surviving bats took to sucking the blood of people and their fowls, a practice that they continue to this very day.

A vampire bat also plays a role in a Bororo Indian legend told to ethnologist C. Levi-Strauss in Brazil. In this story, one of the tribe's ancestors found tobacco in the belly of a fish that he had caught. Not wanting to share his discovery, the Indian hid the fish and secretly smoked the tobacco late at night. His companions, smelling the burning tobacco, demanded that he give them some too. But not knowing how to use tobacco, the men swallowed the smoke instead of inhaling it into their lungs. A vampire bat now appeared, who, after telling the Indians that tobacco was a substance that belonged to him, told them how to smoke properly.

Figure 36. "Killer bat" in the Copán, Honduras Museum. This Maya statue is one of several thought to have adorned the "House of Bats" which has now been destroyed by the encroaching Rió Copán. Note the Maya sign for death on the pendant.

89

VAMPIRE BATS AND PEOPLE

Of the three major Indian civilizations about which we have some knowledge -- the Aztec, Inca, and Maya -- only the Maya occupied prime vampire bat habitat. It is not surprising then, that vampire bats play a significant role in the Popol Vuh, the creation myth of the Quiché Maya. In this legend, passed on from generation to generation, and one of the few accounts to have survived the Conquest, the heroic twin ancestors of the Maya, Xbalanque and Hunahpu, are beset by vampire bats in the cave of the great death bat Cámalzotz who kills and consumes all who enter his lair. Protected by their blow guns, the twins manage to prevent the vampires from biting them until sunrise when the cluster of returning bats lands on the end of Hunahpu's blowgun through which he had been observing the entrance to the cave. His vision thus obscured, Hunahpu succumbs to Cámalzotz who bites off the hero's head.

Bats and bat-god motifs are a common theme in ancient Maya art. Several sculptures of killer-bats, some adorned with the Maya sign (o\°) for death have been found at Copán in Honduras. Adorning so-called "bat houses," which are believed to have been used for the confinement and torment of prisoners, similar figures have been excavated at Tikal, Guatemala, and other locations. Bat glyphs were used as metaphors for sacrifices and the shedding of blood, presumably because of the blood-letting propensities of vampires and predatory bats. Conversely, the Cakchiquel branch of the Maya are said to have adopted the vampire bat as their totem as it represented the god of heaven.

There also appears to be at least one Aztec myth involving a vampire bat. According to one interpretation of the Codex Magliabechiano, a Nahuatal picture book drawn in the 1500s, no less a personage than Quetzalcoatl masterbated on a rock where the Plumed Serpent's sperm was transformed into a vampire bat. This bat was then sent by the gods to bite the flower goddess Xochiquetzal's private parts while she slept. After cutting off her sexual organs, the bat brought them to the gods who washed them. From the water that they spilled came the flowers which now populate the earth.

The Maya and other Indian civilizations, such as the Zapotecs, doubtlessly had a rich lore of legends involving vampire bats as numerous artifacts depicting humans and gods in bat form have been found. Perhaps the most impressive of these are ceramic figures from the Toltec Culture which flourished in what is now Tabasco, Mexico, between 300 and 900 A.D. These two-foot-high statues portray a fierce looking man with vampire-bat-like features standing astride the heads of what appear to be bats, jaguars, and other carnivorous animals. Man into animal transformations are the norm, not the unusual, in many Indian cultures, and it would be interesting to know what these figures represented. Such knowledge might not only reveal how these cultures viewed vampire bats, but which of the vampire bat's attributes they assigned to various aspects of the human character.

Figure 37. Vampire-like effigy standing on what appears to be the head of a leaf-nosed bat. This and several similar statues from the Maya Classic period are thought to have represented greed. Photographed by the author at the Cicom Museum, Villahermosa, Tabasco, Mexico.

Figure 38. Ceramic figures of bat-like animals made by Huastecas Culture peoples who lived in central Vera Cruz, Mexico, between 300 and 900 A.D. These figures are thought to have been used in making music. Photographed by the author at the Cicom Museum in Villahermosa, Tabasco, Mexico.

CONTEMPORARY FOLKLORE

> I am more worried about the wingless and tailless "Cafe au lait," than I am about *Desmodus rufus.* In fact, the only reason for presenting this paper is to ask you to help me tell the mothers of our personnel not to take too seriously the "scare-head" stories of strange exotic diseases like "Bat Rabies."
>
> Colonel Leon A. Fox, U.S. Army Medical
> Bulletin, "Mad Dogs With Wings," 1941

Wherever vampire bats occur there are local superstitions regarding their activities. Most prevalent among these beliefs is the assumption that people who are bitten by bats have been so chosen because of some past misbehavior or that they are cursed in some way. For these reasons, people often deny having been bitten by a vampire bat, even though the marks of the animal's visit are clearly in evidence. Euphemisms are therefore often resorted to when discussing vampire bat bites. "Did the surgeon visit you last night?" was an old inquiry of someone who had been bitten by a vampire bat in British Guiana, referring to the former practice of surgeons bleeding patients for a variety of ailments. So prevalent was this metaphor that vampire bats in the colony were called "Dr. Blairs" after an old-time medico who often prescribed blood-letting as a remedy.

A contemporary Maya euphemism for a girl who has recently been "deflowered" is to say that she has been bitten by a [vampire] bat. The bleeding connotation is obvious. For this same reason the Kógi tribe of Indians in Columbia refer to a girl's first menstrual period as resulting from a visit by a vampire bat.

In some rural areas, especially those having a strong influx of Indian culture, vampire bats are associated with witchcraft. In present day Guatemala vampire bats are regarded as sorcerers who's visits can cause death and disease -- a belief probably linked to the bat's ability to inflict rabies. In a remarkable analog with Old World vampyrism, vampire bats in 17th century Peru were thought to be witches who pierced the bodies of those they wanted to kill and sucked out their blood. Even now, rural Mexicans may ascribe their wounds to having been visited by a *bruja* or witch. Arthur M. Greenhall reports that Blacks and Creoles on the island of Trinidad attribute vampire bat wounds to *soucouyants*, mythical, blood-sucking *jumbies*, or evil spirits. The *soucouyant* is an old woman who sheds her skin at night, usually secreting it under the stone mortar in which she grinds her food. Assuming the form of a ball of fire, she then enters her victim's dwelling through a crack or key-hole where she nourishes herself on the blood of some hapless donor. To rid oneself of such depredations, one visits the *soucouyant's* house, discovers her shed skin, and liberally sprinkles hot pepper on it so that when she puts it back on she burns herself to death. A less lethal preventative, one that is also employed against *brujas* in Mexico, is to seal all cracks and key-holes against entry, and then sprinkle rice or wheat outside the doorway. This compels the *soucouyant* to count every grain before entering the house, a preoccupation that takes until daylight when she loses her supernatural powers for harm.

There are numerous other New World myths involving vampire bat-like spooks or bogeymen. Besides having bat-like features, these imaginary creatures typically possess bat-like attributes. Most descriptions of these spooks are anthropomorphicalogical rather than realistic, that is they have both bat-like and human-like characteristics as well as supernatural ones. They also have a number of bat-like attributes like living in caves or other subterranean recesses, come out only at night, are able to fly, see in the dark, etc. They commonly haunt cemetaries and prey upon travelers at crossroads or women answering a call to nature during the night. Depredations upon women are almost always of a sexual nature. In most legends the spook is fought with fire and light, man's allies against bats and forces of darkness.

The Blackman is a bogeyman of the present day Maya in the highlands of Chiapas in southern Mexico. A winged black-colored demon, the Blackman specializes in unrestrained sexuality, people snatching, and cannibalism. Legends vary from village to village, and teller to teller, but in some versions he has a six foot long, death-dealing penis and can cause his victims to go insane. A typical legend has him carrying off a woman caught out at night to his cave where he either rapes or seduces her. Once a woman has intercourse with a Blackman, often bearing one or more children as a result, there is no way that she can return to her old life in the village. She will forever more have a bad odor about her and her children will have characteristics of the Blackman. To destroy a Blackman one has to either impale, burn, or cook him. Sarah Blaffer, who has extensively researched the Blackman myth, believes that the Blackman Legends have their origin in ancient Maya myths of a ferocious vampire bat demon who possessed many of the same powers and attributes of the Blackman including the ability to transform itself into other creatures.

In a similar vein, ethnologist P.G. Roe tells of a Shipibo legend from the Peruvian jungle in which a woman weds a demon "who is like a man" and wears black. He forbids her to look at him in the daytime, and when she does, she sees how ugly he is with his misshapen "snout and wings." When she leaves her husband and returns home to her family, the bat-demon follows her and kills her by sucking out her blood.

According to M. Wagner, there is a similar legend told on the coast of Ecuador. In this rendition a "Tin-Tin" whistles to adolescent girls on moonlit nights. Should the girl come forth, the Tin-Tin will seduce her and carry her off to his cave where he ravishes and impregnates her.

These myths are surprisingly similar to a story told by Antonio Guzmán, a member of the Desana tribe, a branch of the Tukano Indians living in the Amazonian rain forest. This myth, published in *Amazonian Cosmos*, describes the Uahtí -- hair-covered creatures of the forest and water. The forest Uahtí are the dangerous ones. They are small in stature, human-like in form, large-bellied at times and have feet lacking in toes. Fortunately, their presence is announced by the flurry of bats which constantly accompany them, especially the "large vampire bats." Some Uahtí are said to have an enormous penis and delight in attacking adolescent girls as well as men.

The ability of the vampire bat to inflict a painless bite is still a source of mystery. Many rural people remain convinced that the vampire bat injects an anaesthetic while opening a wound, and the long-held belief that the bat induces a deep sleep by fanning a person's face prior to biting also dies hard. Not a few people are of the opinion that the vampire's bite is venomous, while others fear being bled to death -- reasonable concerns given that some bites have resulted in humans being infected with rabies, and that the anticoagulant in the bat's saliva can result in a copious loss of blood.

There are numerous legends concerning the vampire bat's behavior. Some folks consider the bat to be more carnivorous than sanguinous, and think that these animals are only attracted to blood in the same manner as sharks are said to be. Patricia Morton relayed a story told to her by an old man in Costa Rica who thought that after biting out a divot of flesh from a cow or a horse, the vampire bat flies off to hang this piece of purloined meat in a tree, the bat then feeding on the insects attracted by its putrefying bait. Some villagers contend that several species of bats, if not all bats, are vampires. A case in point is the "Bat Mass Ritual," practiced by two Maya groups in southern Belize. Nominally Catholics, these people raise hogs which are periodically plagued by vampire bats. According to Tim McCarthy, who has worked among these Indians, the villagers will catch a bat (the species doesn't seem to matter) whenever the number of bites on hogs or humans is deemed excessive. A Mass is then said among the villagers and the bat is held or pinned down and prayed over. After telling the bat of their problems, and imploring it to tell the other bats to leave them alone, the bat is released back into the wild.

Some beliefs may yet prove to be true or partially true. Ranchers and biologists have observed that bat bites in several areas become more frequent with the onset of the rainy season, and believe that vampire bat depredations are most severe during wet, "El Niño," years. Some observers in the vampire bat's northern range, and at higher elevations elsewhere, are of the opinion that vampire bats are migratory, the bats abandoning their colder haunts during the winter months. Although the local movement of colonies from winter to summer roosts has been documented, no one has yet demonstrated that vampire bats actually migrate. I doubt that they do as my colleagues and I have netted vampire bats at the northern extremity of their range in southern Sonora in late November as well as in August. Several cases of bovine rabies were also reported from the same vicinity the following January.

In rural Tlaxcala there is a persistent belief in *tlahuelpuchis*, female witches who assume animal form and suck the blood of infants. This ancient Nahuatl form of vampyrism not only explains the unfathomable phenomena of crib death, it helps alleviate the mother of some of her guilt. Usually coming during the wee hours of the morning, the *tlahuelpuchi* typically takes on the form of a turkey, cat, or other animal. But even though ethnologist Hugo Nutini documented 47 reported cases of "blood-sucking" witchcraft in the 1960s, including the execution of an accused *tlahuelpuchi*, none of the reported transformations was said to involve a bat. This is perhaps because the Tlaxcala-Pueblan Valley in which these incidents occurred is at too high an elevation to be good vampire bat habitat. Nonetheless, none of the regional folklore in Latin America that I am aware of has the bat's bite turn anyone into either a vampyre or a vampire bat. Such transformations appear to owe their origins entirely to the introduced European superstition.

VAMPYRES

> After having taken the appropriate action, we ordered heads of all these vampyres to be cut off by some wandering bohemians, their bodies to be burned, and their ashes scattered in the Moravia, while the corpses found to be in a state of decomposition were returned to their coffins. I affirm -- together with the assistant field surgeons despatched to me -- that all these things took place just as we have reported them at Medwegya, in Serbia, on January 7th, 1732.

> Johannes Fluckinger, Regimental Field
> Surgeon (and four others) to Emperor
> Charles VI of Austria-Hungary

Supernatural beings that visit humans and animals during the night to feed on their blood or other life-giving forces are a widespread and persistent belief. Legends of such creatures have been reported for various cultures almost worldwide, including China, India, Malaya, the Phillipines, Arabia, Turkey, Africa, and Europe. The ancient Greeks and Romans told of *lamiae* and *succubi*, demons in female form who sucked men's blood while having sexual relations with them in their sleep until they were deprived of their manhood or died. Their male counterpart was the *incubus* who preyed on women in a like fashion. Similar creatures are found in Oriental legends with the added attraction that they fed on corpses as well as blood. Nor were such beliefs confined to the Eastern Hemisphere. Prior to the Conquest, the Aztec Indians of Mexico had a dread of dead women called *Ciuateteos*. *Ciuateteos* could be the most lascivious of succubi or hideous hags, both of which sought out young men in order to copulate with them, some even bearing children as a result.

The blood-sucking *vampyre* best known to Westerners has its origins in ancient Assyria and goes back to at least Babylonian times. Like their Mediterranean *laminae* and *succubi* counterparts, these Middle-eastern ghouls were undead creatures who subsisted upon the blood and flesh of the living. Oftentimes on their nightly visits they took the form of "night birds" -- owls and bats, bats then being considered to be birds. More often, however, these transformations took the form of wolves, cats, and other animals, or even straw, beams of light, or wisps of smoke. A particularly worrisome aspect was that anyone preyed upon by one of these vampyres, became one himself. Hence, vampyre attacks rapidly blossomed into epidemics. In order to put a halt to their depredations, it was necessary to find each of the vampyres' graves, dig up their undecomposed bodies, and drive wooden stakes through their hearts. Beheading, and burning the bodies and hearts of any vampyres found was also highly recommended.

Such legends spread throughout the Near East, through Turkey to Macedonia, and into the Balkans. For religious and other reasons, the vampyre superstition became particularly entrenched among the Slavic and other Eastern Orthodox Christian peoples of Turkish occupied Europe. Here the ancient legends were promulgated and embellished until the fear of vampyres literally became a way of life and death. Vampyres in a variety of forms were often blamed for any unexplainable event, especially the sudden deaths of people and animals. By the late 1600s and early 1700s, waves of vampyre hysteria were being reported from various parts of eastern Europe, most commonly in the fiefdoms of Wallachia, Moldavia, Serbia, and Transylvania. One of the most notable of these epidemics was what became renown as the Arnold Paole case.

Hearing of yet another outbreak of vampyrism, this time near the village of Medwegya in Serbia, the Austrian government decided to send a contingent of medical examiners under Field Surgeon Johannes Fluckinger to investigate. Having acquired parts of Serbia and Wallachia in 1718 under the Treaty of Passarowitz, the Roman Catholic Austrians were upset over reports of dead bodies being dug up, stakes being driven through their hearts, and the corpses being dismembered and cremated. On arriving in Medwegya in December 1731 the Emperor's medical officers were told of a number of recent deaths in the area, and that at least some of these deaths were thought to be due to a self-confessed vampyre named Arnold Paole who had "died" of a broken neck five years previously. Several persons had complained of being tormented by Paole some twenty to thirty days after his supposed death, and when his grave was examined, his body was found to be perfectly preserved. What was more, his eyes were filled with blood, and blood was also flowing from his ears and nose. His fingernails and toenails had dropped off, and new ones had grown in to take their place. When a stake was driven through his heart, he was said to have given a loud shriek, and great quantities of blood had gushed forth. His remains were then burned and the ashes returned to his tomb.

Unfortunately for the local populace, Paole was thought to have attacked several people as well as cattle prior to being discovered.

Therefore, it was believed, the arch-vampyre was still at work by proxy. Although the corpses of his human victims had undergone the anti-vampyre treatment, all the villagers who had eaten beef from cattle that had been fed upon by the vampyres were now presumed to be vampyres themselves. Seventeen people had recently died within a three month span, some of them mysteriously. At least some of the deaths were assumed to be the delayed work of Paole.

As Fluckinger and his officers watched, 15 corpses were disintered and examined, including two children dead for eight and 18 days, respectively. According to Fluckinger's account, 11 of the bodies were "judged to be in a vampyre state," including a 60 year-old woman, who, despite having been buried for 90 days, was much plumper than she had been in life, and whose breasts were full of liquid blood. It was said that she had eaten mutton contaminated by vampyres. Another woman, who had claimed to have been visited by one of the village's vampyres, bore the telltale marks -- "under her left ear, we could clearly make out a bluish scar, from which blood had been sucked." And so it went, each of the 11 bodies displaying signs of being preserved by nights of blood-sucking.

Fluckinger's eye-witness report caused an immense sensation on his return to Vienna. Copies were immediately translated and printed throughout Europe where it captured the imagination of common folk and crowned heads of government alike. Everyone, clergymen, scholars, even the new men of science, had an explanation for the strange events taking place in eastern Europe. Vampyrism became an obsession, and in 1734 the word "vampyre" made its way into the English Oxford dictionary. It was only natural then, that when supposed blood-sucking bats began arriving in European collections from South America and the Far East, Linnaeus, reportedly on the suggestion of the French naturalist Buffon, named them vampyres.

Meanwhile, vampyre outbreaks continued to plague eastern Europe. Vampyre epidemics were reported in Silesia in 1755, in Romania in 1756, and in Russia in 1772, and so on into the first half of the 19th Century. Even now, ignorant and superstitious people continue to believe in vampyres. Vampyre exorcisms are still practiced by the Eastern Orthodox Church, and as recently as 1974, nearly 100 vampyre-hunters converged on Highgate Cemetery outside London in search of a seven-foot vampyre that had been seen stalking the graveyard. After breaking into tombs and driving an iron stake into a number of corpses, David Farrant, the leader of the party, was arrested and sentenced to five years in prison for desecrating the dead. While such overt incidents are rare, many people remain fascinated with the vampyre mystique whether they actually believe in vampyres or not.

Of the numerous "experts" who have researched the vampyre myth, and analyzed the reasons for its continued existence and popularity, the most famous is undoubtedly an English cleric named Montague Sumners. In his books, *The Vampire: His Kith and Kin*, and *The Vampire In Europe*, Sumners not only tells you how to dispose of vampyres, but how to recognize one. Eerily, not a few of these traits can also be ascribed to the vampire bat -- "puffed and bloated after feeding;" "teeth white and gleaming,.. notably sharp and pointed;" "often hare-lipped;" "nails, curved, crooked, and long;" "sharp-pointed tongue;" "excessive strength and agility;" "sees in the dark;" "hair often a peculiar shade of red;" "shrieks and screams when agitated;" "sexually rapacious;" "able to bite its victim without awakening him or her." Add to these characteristics, the often stated testimony that a vampyre's lair has a fetid odor, and you have a series of very bizarre coincidences indeed. Given these similarities, the transformation of vampyres into vampire bats, while largely a recent embellishment on the vampyre legend, is perfectly logical. Yet, Sumners and his predecessors lacked any intimate knowledge of vampire bats. Does fact indeed imitate fiction? One has to wonder.

VAMPYRISM AND REAL-LIFE VAMPYRES

> From that time on, he sought in every possible way to see and, where practicable, to taste the fresh blood of females. That of young girls was preferred by him. He spared no pains or expense to obtain this pleasure.

> Richard van Krafft-Ebing, Case 28. J. H.,
> aged 26, *Psychopathia Sexualis*, 1883

Why is the vampyre myth so popular and persistent? To answer this question, one must understand that myths are usually attempts to explain the unexplainable. In hindsight we can now see that there are pathological, physiological, psychopathic, and even psychological reasons for a belief in vampyres.

Many, perhaps all, of Eastern Europe's vampyre episodes appear to have coincided with epidemics of deadly diseases. Not knowing about microbes, it was only natural that medieval people attributed sudden deaths to supernatural forces. Since relatives of the deceased were often the next to go, death itself came to be regarded as a contagious affliction -- deaths that were as logically spread by vampyres as by any other method then known. Descriptions of events leading up to a wave of vampyre hysteria are often symptomatic of bubonic plague, cholera, or rabies. The odor of death commonly attributed to vampyre victims is a sign of plague. Similarly, reports of people suffering irrational, and oftentimes violent behavior, followed by an agonizing death after being bitten by a wolf or other animal are symptoms of rabies. Wasting away, a common fate of vampyre victims, is indicative of several diseases. Consumptives, especially, were thought to be suffering from the attentions of vampyres.

Premature burial of unembalmed bodies was not uncommon during times of pestilence. Ergo, the reports of bodies moving in their coffins and eating their burial shrouds have a natural if macabre explanation. Placing a corpse in cold volcanic soil, or in a cool vault, also greatly slows the decomposition process, as does burial itself (by a factor of 8). Bodies can appear to remain in a state of preservation for days and even weeks after being placed in the ground. Forensic science also now tells us that many of the characteristics observed in interred "vampyres" are not that unusual. Rigor mortis relaxes with decomposition; fingernails fall off, leaving the old nail beds looking like new nails; hair appears to grow as the skin naturally retracts; blood in a body can not only remain fluid for weeks, it expands with decomposition to seep from the mouth and other orifices. Thus the corpses of "vampyres" are said to be bloated and ruddy in color, with the fresh blood of last night's victim frequently on their mouths. Gases too, form in every decaying body, and can cause the corpse to "moan and groan," and, if penetrated by a stake or other object, the corpse can emit a shriek, and can even sit-up in its coffin.

Dreams and other psychic phenomena (again frequently involving departed relatives), undoubtedly account for a number of vampyre visitations. Certain individuals also suffer from porphyria, a malady that causes them to be anaemic and sensitive to sunlight. Such people are naturally pale, and interestingly, are said to have a negative reaction to garlic -- another common trait of vampyres.

Psychological factors provide additional explanations for the belief in vampyres. Drawing blood, or the sight of blood, is a source of sexual arousal for some people, and biting and scratching are recommended love-making techniques in the Kama Sutra. To those who engage in such behavior, blood-letting can range from mild-sexual play, through S-M activities such as flogging, to the commission of monstrous crimes. Oftentimes blood is ingested in what may or may not be a means of sexual gratification. Individuals practicing these fetishes in medieval times would naturally arouse suspicion as to their motives and be considered "vampyres" by the general populace. Such people, however, are vampyrists, not vampyres. That is, they consume blood, but have no extraordinary abilities.

Vampyrists may be male or female, heterosexual or homosexual. Their activities include performing cunnilingus on a woman during her menstrual cycle, biting themselves or their partner until blood is drawn, collecting their's or someone else's blood with a hypodermic syringe, and pricking each other's fingers or skin with an auto-lancet -- an over-the-counter scalpel used by diabetics. Auto-vampyrists, those who cut themselves, tend to be women, while taking blood from others is more likely to be a male activity. These people often belong to clubs which cater to these fetishes and those that supply the blood consider themselves to be donors rather than victims.

Much more terrifying are psychopathic vampyrists, people having an irresistible compulsion to obtain blood by means of force. These people are definitely psychotic and, like some schizophrenics, may not recognize themselves in a mirror. They commonly have a morbid obsession with death, and frequently dream of blood and suffering. Their reaction to blood may be sexual or asexual, and they are almost always men who show no outward signs of mental illness. Both self-mutilation and the mutilation of others may be involved, and the psychosis is usually progressive. Thankfully, this form of vampyrism is rare, but some of history's more notable examples have undoubtedly contributed to vampyre legends through the ages. Nor is it an accident that some of the most famous cases took place in those lands having the richest heritage of vampyre lore.

One of the earliest known and most notorious vampyrists was Gilles de Rais, a Marshal of France who fought alongside Joan d'Arc. Tried in 1440 for slitting the throats of 400 children, it was thought that he may have murdered twice as many. His *modus operandi* was to have his servants stab a youth in the jugular vein in such a manner that the blood would spurt on his person. After testimony that he sat on the bowels of a dying boy while drinking his blood, he was executed by strangulation and his body burned.

Countess Elisabeth Bathory of Transylvania is almost unique in being one of the few criminal women vampyrists. Believing that bathing in the blood of buxom young girls maintained a youthful complexion, the countess hired a progression of servant girls which she and her handmaidens imprisoned, tortured, and killed. The numbers of deaths attributed to her atrocities range from 40 to as high as 650. With strong lesbian overtones, the countess is reported to have had her attendants lick the blood off of her back rather than use towels. After a sensational trial in 1611, her accomplices were burned alive after having their fingernails pulled out. The Countess, being of noble birth, was immune from execution, however. Instead, she was sealed inside of her castle to spend the remainder of her days in enforced solitude. She died after only three years of seclusion.

Of more recent vintage was Fritz Haarman, "The Hanover Vampyre," who is believed to have killed about 50 boys and young men in post-World-War-I Germany. His victims were lured to his home, usually with the aid of an accomplice, entrapped, and killed by biting them in the jugular vein. After drinking their blood, the bodies were often ground up into sausage which Haarman then ate or sold. Haarman, in true vampyre fashion, was beheaded for his crimes in 1924.

John Haigh, the infamous "acid-bath" murderer was hung in 1949 after confessing to killing nine people. Although his victims were also robbed, Haigh claimed that his primary motive was his insatiable desire for blood. He would shoot or club his prey in the head, some of whom were his acquaintances, plug their wounds, and then incise their necks. Then he would draw a cupful of blood and drink it. After doing so, the Englishman stated that he would feel "relieved."

A more recent example was a deaf-mute German laborer named Kuno Hoffman. After reading their obituaries in the newspaper, Hoffman broke into the graves of at least 35 deceased persons. He stabbed the corpses with knives or sliced them with razors, and then drank their blood to make himself "good-looking and strong." Sometimes he cut off their heads or cut out their hearts. His downfall came after he was apprehended for killing a live couple in a lover's lane and drinking their blood from the gun-shot wounds -- blood, which he declared to be much better than that of corpses!

Less dangerous perhaps, but equally bizarre, was the case of Demetrious Myicura, a Polish immigrant who was found dead in his London flat in 1973. The man apparently had an obsessive fear of vampyres and had attempted to make his room "vampyre-proof" by placing bowls of salt and garlic mixed with urine at strategic entryways. Salt was scattered on everything, including his blankets, and he slept with a clove of garlic in his mouth. But the vampyre got him in the end; an autopsy showed that he had choked to death on the garlic bulb which had lodged in his throat after he had finally gone to sleep!

Clearly, there are things far more worrisome than mere vampire bats. That this bat has come to be even remotely associated with these hideous legends and practices is an unfortunate if understandable coincidence of natural and unnatural history.

VAMPYRES AND VAMPIRE BATS IN WESTERN LITERATURE

> But first, on earth as vampire sent,
> Thy corpse shall from its tomb be rent:
> Then ghastly haunt thy native place,
> And suck the blood of all thy race.

> Lord George Gordon Byron, *Giaour*, 1813

Vampire bats were not always linked to vampyres. Indeed, the role of bats in Eastern European vampyre legends was originally a minor one. Romanian peasants believed that a bat flying over a corpse could cause it to become a vampyre, and that vampyres occasionally assumed the form of a bat. But wolves, cats, and other animals were more likely guises for vampyre transformations, as vampire bats were obviously unknown in the region. Only later, and only because of Western embellishments on the vampyre legends of Eastern Europe, would vampire bats become associated with vampyres.

Figure 39. Seventeenth century engraving of a "vampire bat." Note the cat-like face and human body form.

Vampyre tales first became popular in Europe in the 1700s with the publication of Austrian and German texts on what had heretofore been largely an Eastern phenomenon. Fluckinger's report on the Arnold Paole case was avidly read, not only in Austria, but throughout the continent. Having gone through several translations and versions, some of them highly sensational, it was only a matter of time before vampyres became a popular fictional theme. A favorite twist was to portray the vampyre as a creature of noble birth, an allusion popular with the general public as it provided a convenient means of illustrating the blood-sucking propensities of royalty with a minimum of risk. Naturally, the locale for most of these works was somewhere in the Balkans -- a setting that would return again and again throughout the history of the genre. Accordingly, bats played almost no part in the telling of these tales which were essentially ghost stories.

Figure 40. Drawing of a half man-half vampire bat monster reported to have been discovered in Chile. Rendition of a 1784 newspaper illustration by Randy Babb.

Vampire bats and vampire-bat-like monsters were meanwhile claiming their own share of printer's ink. Reports of the discovery of blood-sucking bats, not only in the jungles of South America, but throughout the world, made good copy with those starved to hear more of the world's newly discovered wonders. To the arm-chair explorer, almost no report seemed too incredulous to be believed. One of the most fantastic examples was the capture in Chile of a giant half man, half vampire bat creature reported in the October 1784 issue of a Parisian tabloid, the *Courier de L'Europa*. Not only was the account widely accepted as true, an expedition was said to be underway to secure a female of the species so that the pair could be bred and exhibited in a zoological garden! Not willing to wait to see such an oddity in the flesh, a brisk trade developed in artistic renditions of what was widely accepted as only the latest in a series of natural wonders that already included such oddities as the giraffe, rhinoceros, and dodo bird. Also lending credence to such a "discovery" was the accepted idea that cross-breeding different kinds of animals, including man, was possible, if highly unnatural. What the basis, if any, of this "discovery" was is hard to say, perhaps the capture of one of the species of bats with "man-like" facial features.

The greatest impetus for vampyre stories, however, had its origins in the same wet summer of 1816 which also saw the genesis of *Frankenstein*. Here, in a chalet on the coast of Lake Geneva, Lord Byron, his young physician John Polidori, Percival Bysshe Shelly, Mary Godwin Shelly, and Claire Clairmont (Mary's stepsister), took time out from their cavortings to read gothic horror stories including some of the recently available texts on Eastern European vampyres. After loading themselves up with laudanum and eating tainted meat to induce nightmares, the little group decided that they should each write their own ghost story. One result, besides Mary Shelly's classic novel *Frankenstein*, was Polidori's *The Vampyre*, originally published in 1819 under Byron's name. *The Vampyre*, in which the noble Lord Ruthven plays a vampyre sucking the life blood of his hapless victims, was an immediate success, so much so that it spawned a series of gentlemanly vampyre imitators. One of the most popular, if not the least literate of these, was the serialized *Varney the Vampyre* or *The Feast of Blood* which appeared in 1847. Termed a "penny-dreadful," because of the genre's cheap prices and hack writing style, even the novel's authorship is uncertain, most researchers now believing the writer to be Thomas Prest. Whoever the author was, *Varney* sold the common folk on the vampyre myth, and accelerated the trend toward more and longer vampyre novels. Eventually, many of Europe's most famous 19th century authors got in on the vampyre bandwagon in one form or another -- Goethe, Alexandre Dumas, Alexis Tolstoy (Leo's cousin), Guy de Maupassant, H.G. Wells, Arthur Conan Doyle, and Jules Verne to name only a few. But while some of the tales, like Sheridan Le Fanu's *Carmilla*, starred a female vampyre, the bat motif was left largely to the illustrators of their works.

Ironically, one of the first books to incorporate the bat image is neither about traditional vampyres nor vampire bats. Sir Richard Burton's *Vikrum and the Vampire*, first published in 1870, is a collection of ancient Sanskrit folk tales featuring an Indian vampyre or *baital* who animates dead bodies, and hangs from the boughs of a tree like a bat. The bat guise of Burton's *baital* is nonetheless weak, although considerably strengthened in his wife's preface in the second, "memorial" edition of 1893 in which Isabel describes the *baital* as a "huge bat" looking rather like a flying fox. This posthumous edition is also charmingly illustrated by drawings of bat-like night creatures by Ernest Giset.

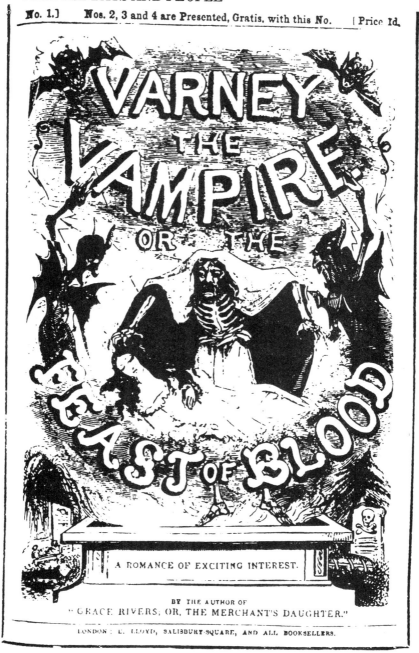

No. 1.] Nos. 2, 3 and 4 are Presented, Gratis, with this No. [Price 1d.

A ROMANCE OF EXCITING INTEREST.

BY THE AUTHOR OF
" GRACE RIVERS, OR, THE MERCHANT'S DAUGHTER."

LONDON : E. LLOYD, SALISBURY-SQUARE, AND ALL BOOKSELLERS.

Figure 41. Title page of an early printing of *Varney the Vampire*.

Figure 42. Illustration of vampyre scene by Gustave Doré for Dante's *Divine Comedy*.

With the publication of Bram Stoker's *Dracula* in 1897, the vampyre mystique reached a new height from which it has never descended. Stoker's well-crafted story, based on a real 15th Century Romanian nobleman, Vlad Tepes, has never been out of print. Although Vlad Tepes, also known as Vlad the Impaler, was indeed a villain of monstrous proportions, he was neither a vampyre nor a vampyrist. No matter, Stoker made Dracula a vampyre and the two are now almost synonymous in the numerous versions of Stoker's ever popular tale. *Dracula* is also the first vampyre story to ease into the bat transformation role:

...he can command all the meaner things: the rat and the owl, and the bat -- the moth, and the fox, and the wolf; he can grow and become small; and he can at times vanish and come unknown.

and:

But my very feelings changed to repulsion and terror when I saw the whole man slowly emerge...and begin to crawl down the castle wall over that dreadful abyss, *face down*, with his cloak spreading out around him like great wings...

What manner of man is this, or what manner of creature is it in the semblance of man?

Figure 43. Illustration by Ernest Giset in the 1893 edition of Richard Burton's *Vikrum and the Vampire.*

To complete the bat-like image, almost all of the 27 plus editions of Stoker's *Dracula* came generously illustrated with bats and bat-like creatures. With increasing publicity of the vampire bat as a blood-drinker, the images of vampyres and vampire bats became so closely linked as to be almost synonymous.

Figure 44. Copy of a drawing on the cover of the first paperback edition of Bram Stoker's *Dracula*, 1897.

The vampire bat has also come into its own as a literary subject. In addition to such scientific treatises as Dennis Turner's *The Vampire*

VAMPIRE BATS AND PEOPLE

Bat -- a field study in behavior and ecology and Arthur Greenhall's and Uwe Schmidt's definitive compendium, *Natural History of Vampire Bats*, several noteworthy works feature fictional vampire bats. Undoubtedly the most successful novel in this regard is Martin Cruz Smith's million-selling *Nightwing* about rabid vampire bats invading the Hopi and Navajo Indian reservations in Arizona. Another best-seller, Cormac McCarthy's *Blood Meridian*, has the protagonist attacked by a vampire bat while crossing Mexico's Chihuahuan Desert. That vampire bats are considerably out of their range in such works is probably no more unusual than vampyres moving out of Transylvania.

The 20th Century has seen literally hundreds of Dracula, vampyre, and vampire bat publications in every conceivable media, fiction as well as non-fiction -- novels, short stories, stage plays, films, serials, anthologies, television series, documentaries, you name it. There are even cookbooks and songs about vampyres and vampire bats. Oddly enough, at least two dozen children's books are about vampyres, not to mention such cartoon characters as Marvel Comic's "Vampire Tales" and "Dracula," D. C. Comic's "Vampire," and Warren Publishing Company's "Vampirella." The settings include not only eastern Europe, but virtually every country on earth as well as outer space. Many of these tales involve vampire bats or are at least illustrated with bats meant to be vampire bats. Not atypical of these offerings is "Drink My Red Blood," a 1951 short story featuring a boy who becomes fixated by the Dracula legend and steals a vampire bat from the zoo in his efforts to become a vampyre.

So pervasive is the interest in vampyres and vampyrism that several organizations have sprung up to inform their members of vampyrist goings-on and act as clearing houses for vampyre literature and other events. Some of these organizations such as *Nightwing* have newsletters with titles incorporating vampire bat themes. One, an S-M club, even has a newsletter entitled *Desmodus, Inc.*

Vampyres and Vampire Bats on Film

No use wasting your bullets, Martin. They cannot harm that bat.

Dracula, 1931

Perhaps because of their eerie visual impact, bats quickly made the transition from illustrating written works on vampyres to being featured on the big screen. One of the first moving pictures is *Le Manour du Diable* (The Devil's Manor) produced by Georges Melies in 1897. Lasting a brief three minutes, this French film shows a large bat flying into a gothic castle, where it circles about, and then magically changes into Mephistopheles. By waving a wand, the Devil then makes a beautiful woman appear. Finally, a man arrives, and after brandishing a crucifix, causes the Devil to disappear. In another film by the same producer in 1903, *Le Puits Fantastique* (The Enchanted Well), the Devil transforms himself into a bat, thus bringing the bat transformation process full circle. Yet another French film, *The Vampire* (1914), has a psychologist attempt to kill his wife with narcotics and the aid of a super-sized "vampire bat."

Most "vampire" movies of the 1910s and 1920s, star neither vampyres nor vampire bats but psychic *vamps* like Theda Bara, beautiful women who entice, seduce, and then destroy their lovers. Although a number of silent movies produced both in the U.S. and in foreign countries feature vampyres, few if any, appear to have capitalized on the bat transformation theme. This includes the still popular German film *Nosferatu* (1922) starring Max Schreck. Heavily based on Bram Stoker's *Dracula* without credit or authorization, this truly spooky film contains no bats or bat transformations, using instead scenes of scurrying rats and the effects of plague to instill a sense of horror and dread.

Not until the release of the original movie version of *Dracula* in 1931 did the bat finally assume its role as an integral part of the vampyre legend. More of a rendition of the stage play than the novel, this film, starring Bela Lugosi, remains the quintessential vampyre film. Not only do the movie's opening credits appear against a bat logo, Dracula appears in bat form no fewer than seven times. Besides the memorable scene in which a bat leads the stagecoach's horses from Birgau Pass to Castle Dracula, the Count uses his bat transformation guise to gain access to both Lucy's and Mina's bedrooms and to escape when pressed too close. Never, however, does the viewer see the bat transformation process which always occurs offscreen.

Never believing in too much of a good thing, Hollywood employed vampire bats to draw audiences in several movies in the 1930s and 1940s. These included *The Vampire Bat* (1932) in which a mad doctor in a Balkan village tries to cover up his weird experiments by fomenting a vampire bat scare, as well as several *Dracula* sequels also starring Bela Lugosi. One of these, *Son of Dracula* (1943), is notable in that, for the first time, a victim is attacked by Count Alucard (Dracula spelled backwards) while in bat form. A more creative theme was explored in *Condemned to Live* (1935) in which a pregnant woman is bitten by a vampire bat in Africa with the result that her offspring turns into a vampire-like werewolf on nights having a full moon. In *The Devil Bat* (1940), also starring Bela Lugosi, and later called *The Killer Bat*, a disgruntled scientist uses electricity to enlarge vampire bats (actually a stuffed flying fox perched on a coathanger) until they are the size of dogs. He then sics them on his employer's family by applying a special

111

scent to their persons. Bad as this movie is, and it is bad, it proved lucrative enough to generate a sequel, *The Devil Bat's Daughter* (1946).

From Paul Landres's THE VAMPIRE

Figure 45. Poster advertising United Artist's 1957 movie, *The Vampire*.

The 1950s were a heyday for vampyre movies and every country with a film industry appears to have produced at least one example -- Mexico, Brazil, Malaya, Turkey and Italy, as well as England and the U.S. Mexican entries included the highly camp *El Vampiro* (1956), and in 1959, *El Ataud del Vampiro* (The Vampire's Coffin). In the latter film the vampyre is destroyed in bat form by a spear being thrown through his body. In what is probably the best of the Mexican vampyre movies, *Nostradamus* (1960), the vampyre assumes bat form when threatened by the sign of the cross. Having neither vampire bats nor a strong vampyre mythology, the enterprising Japanese produced *Kyuketsu Ga* (The Vampire Moth). Italian movie-makers, well known

112

for heroic epics, countered with *Goliath and The Vampires* (1961), which if the advertisements can be believed, featured battles with truly gigantic vampire bats. In an unusual American entry, *The Mark of the Vampire* (1957), a doctor unwittingly takes pills made of bat serum to become a sympathetic if not pathetic vampyre. More prophetic was *It!* - - *The Terror From Beyond Space* (1958) which heralded a new genre of science-fiction films featuring vampyres and vampire bats in outer space.

The number of vampyre movies exploded after 1960 until there are now close to 1000 titles. By the end of 1993 more than 200 versions had been made of *Dracula* alone. Vampyre movies have also become progressively more violent and graphic, and not a few are pornographic. Along with this trend, the role of the bat, at least malevolent ones, has also waned. There are several reasons for this. For one thing, real-life bats are no longer regarded as particularly threatening by most movie-goers, and bat imagery is now more mysterious and foreboding than the bats themselves. Bats are also not particularly vivid in technicolor, and the increasing use of seductive female vampyres does not readily lend itself to transformations into vampire bats.

There have nonetheless been some notable exceptions to the decreasing use of bats as creatures of horror. Posters hyping *Kiss of the Vampire* (1963), a British film, show the stars being attacked by bats. In the *Scars of Dracula* (1970), one of several of Hammer Film's Dracula movies starring Christopher Lee, bat transformations are not only used to good effect, it is a bat that kills the villagers. In another relatively sophisticated English movie, *Vampire Circus* (1971), acrobats impress the audience by turning into bats. *Horrors of the Blood Monsters* (1970), has a vampyre plague infect Earth from a planet inhabited by vampyric batmen. In a more humorous vein, *Dracula (The Dirty Old Man)* (1969) has Dracula living in a cave with his mother, a rubber vampire bat! Another X-rated movie, *The Case of the Full Moon Murders* (1974), stars a girl who, besides performing oral sex when the moon is full, is capable of turning herself into a vampire bat.

Mexican movie-makers also appear to have been reluctant to abandon both vampyres and vampire bats. At any rate the 1960s and early 1970s saw a stream of Mexican movies with titles such as *El Vampiro Sangriento* (*The Bloody Vampire*, 1961), *La Sombra del Murciélago* (*The Bat's Shadow*, 1966), *Las Vampiras* (*The Female Vampires*, 1968), *El Vampireo y El Sexo* (*The Vampire and Sex*, 1968), and *Chanoc Contra El Tigre y El Vampiro* (*Chanoc Against the Jaguar and the Vampire*, 1971). In *Las Luchadores Contra La Momia* (*Lady Wrestlers Versus The Mummy*) the producers push all of their country's cultural buttons by having women wrestlers take on an Aztec mummy that turns into a vampire bat.

Outside of the vampyre venue, there have been such American films as *It Lives By Night* or *The Bat People* (1973), in which a man exploring a cave is bitten by a vampire bat with the result that he becomes one himself. Other bat films include *Nightwing* (1978), Columbia's screen adaptation of the popular Martin Cruz Smith novel, and *Cujo*, a movie version of a Stephen King thriller featuring a rabid bat that bites a family's Saint Bernard dog with calamitous results. Bat transformations are used to good effect in a fun spoof starring George Hamilton and Susan Saint James entitled *Love At First Bite* in which Dracula bites his victims while in bat form and the two lovers fly off together as vampire bats. In *The Lost Boys* teenage vampyres at least roost like bats, and in Francis Ford Coppola's remake of *Dracula* a grotesque bat-like vampyre is created through the magic of special effects. Two other recent releases, *Batman* and *Batman Returns* also use bat symbolism among a hodge-podge of animal props. In the latter film, catwoman (Michelle Pfieffer) mouths and spits out a bat, and the Penguin (Danny DeVito) releases hordes of supposed vampire bats on Gotham City at Christmastime. A recent British entry, Lifeforce (1985), has astronauts encountering gigantic vampire bats in outer space, and Londoner's, including Patrick Stewart of *Star Trek: the Next Generation* fame, battling a voluptuous female vampyre who spends much of the movie cavorting in the nude!

Interestingly, the only movie to feature real vampire bats is the French documentary *Le Vampire*. This rarely seen film was made in the Gran Chaco of South America in 1943 and shows actual footage of vampire bats stalking their prey and drinking blood.

Vampyres and Vampire Bats on Television: Vampyres and vampire bats quickly adapted to the television screen although at the cost of losing much of their ominous nature. *Dark Shadows*, in which Barnabas did his traveling in bat-form, was an extremely popular soap opera serial in the early 1970s as was the adventures of a civic-minded *Batman*. Late night movie hosts made up like vampyres, and often accompanied by bat props, also proved to be a highly attractive means of introducing horror movies. Sexy female vampyres were the most favored, and such mistresses of the night as Vampira (Marla Nurmi) and Elvira (Cassandra Peterson) achieved considerable fame in the process. Except for occasional nature shows, however, including an excellent documentary on vampire bat control, real vampire bats rarely make it into the living room. When vampyres or vampire bats do appear on television, it is often as benign caricatures in cartoon form whose mission is to teach pre-school children how to count (Sesame Street's The Count) or eat pre-sweetened breakfast cereal (Count Chocula).

THE VAMPIRE BAT AS A LOGO

The vampire, however, is the most harmless of all bats, and its inoffensive character is well known to residents on the banks of the Amazon.

H. W. Bates, 1862, *The Naturalist on the River Amazons*

Even though bats and bat-like figures have been used to depict death and the netherworld throughout history, the vampire bat was not specifically identified as a particularly troublesome character until relatively recent times. As a consequence, most portrayals of vampire bats are generic bat figures with a pair of prominent fangs attached, or, the animal represented is another species of bat entirely. Nor is the bat trademark shown on Bacardi rum bottles since 1862 a vampire bat as is commonly supposed. The animal displayed is actually meant to be a fruit bat which better befits the Cuban origin of the product it sells. It was not until the 20th Century, and the nearly universal exposure of Europeans and Americans to Dracula and his tropical real-life counterpart, that the vampire bat took on a specific identity as a symbol of night-time death and destruction from a loss of blood and disease.

Figure 46. B-25J with a caricature of a vampire bat painted on its nose. Drawing by Randy Babb.

It was only appropriate then that imaginative World War II pilots adopted a vampire bat insignia on night-fighting airplanes. Not only did German and Finnish crews decorate their Messerschmidt Me-109s with vampire bat logos for combat against their Slavic opponents, Allied pilots also incorporated various vampire bat emblems for use on their aircraft. A vampire bat insignia identified P-61 "Black Widow" nightfighters of the U.S. Army Air Force's 6th Night Fighter Squadron based on Saipan, and the nose of at least one B-25J of the 499th Bomb Squadron in Okinawa was decorated with a vampire bat in the style of the renowned "Flying Tigers." One of the first jet fighters, the British De Havilland "Vampire," was the first allied plane to achieve a speed of 500 miles-per-hour. So successful was the "Vampire," and its variants that by 1952 the plane was in service in no fewer than fourteen countries.

Figure 47. Vampire bat in piñata-form used to advertise Halloween treats.

Not all vampire symbols came with an ominous message. Employing a reverse applique technique, women of Panama's Cuna Indian tribe make colorful blouses called *molas*, the backs of which are decorated with various designs and patterns including portrayals of local animals. Arthur Greenhall, in *The Natural History of Vampire Bats*, shows a photograph of a *mola* adorned with what is obviously meant to be a vampire bat. In the same book, Greenhall also tells of bat costumes worn by the people of Trinidad and Tobago during Carnival time. Some of these had wings that opened and closed, and could be easily identified as being vampire bats by their pronounced teeth. Prizes were offered for the best costume, and the owner would show the

116

judges real bats preserved in rum to impress them with the authenticity of his or her masquerade. Stores in both the U.S. and Mexico display *piñatas* that are meant to emulate vampire bats as well as the Batman cartoon character.

Figure 48. *"Abajo Los Vampiros"* (Down the Vampires) logo of the U.S. Aid for International Development.

Figure 49. Vampire bat novelty made in the Philippines (note the projecting fangs). When squeezed the animal emits an eerie tune and the eyes flash red. Photo by author.

117

A more serious application was the use of a vampire bat logo by the U.S. Agency for International Development in its "Abajo Los Vampiros" (Down With Vampire Bats) campaign of the 1970s. Cooperators were issued pins and bumper stickers displaying a slash through a generic bat to advertise the goal of the participants. Today, depictions of bats, at least some of which are intended to be vampires, are most often used to illustrate greeting cards, posters and favors commemorating Halloween parties and other nocturnal gatherings.

Figure 50. Hallmark card of a "Vampire bat" to be used as a sign announcing the location of a Halloween party.

PRESENT STATUS AND ATTITUDE TOWARD VAMPIRE BATS

> In the evening we received a call from the local magnates. It was quite amusing to see their long faces, expressive of a holy horror at our temerity, and they soon added another item to the already formidable list of woes to come, namely vampire bats, that were said to exist in such numbers in a part of the valley of the Sapao, about sixteen miles away, that it is there impossible for any animal to live through the night.
>
> James W. Wells, *Three Thousand Miles Through Brazil*, 1887

There is little question but that the vampire bat has greatly expanded both its numbers and distribution since livestock were introduced to the New World. It is also generally agreed upon that man's attempts to eliminate vampire bats have had little long term effect on the animal's numbers. Despite years of effort, and numerous prognostications on their total eradication, these bats are still present on the island of Trinidad and in other areas where control programs have long been in effect. In fact, no expert now thinks that these bats have totally disappeared anywhere. Unlike the wolf and the grizzly bear, on which man has also waged a relentless war, the vampire bat continues to persist and even thrive. Intelligent, and blessed with a good memory, this "smart bat" has proven itself to be the tropical equivalent of the coyote. As such, the vampire bat is one of the New World's most adaptable and successful native animals.

Nor is the vampire likely to diminish in numbers in the foreseeable future. On the contrary, there is every indication that the species is still expanding its range into new areas due to the accelerated modification of tropical habitats and the introduction of livestock into formerly virgin landscapes. We may as well learn to live with *el vampiro*. We probably have no other choice.

REFERENCES AND BIBLIOGRAPHY

... I want to conclude with depredating bats. I say that in [Panama] there are many of them, and that they were very dangerous to the Christians when they were first transported to the lands of governor V. N. de Balboa after the Darien was conquered. Because of not knowing an easy and safe remedy for the bat's bite, some Christians died and others were in danger of dying until it was learned from the Indians how those bitten could be cured.

Fernando De Oviedo, 1526
(Translated by Barry Spicer)

The following books and articles contain references to vampire bats and vampyrism. Although extensive, this bibliography is by no means complete and only a few examples of the large and important body of foreign language sources are included. Also missing are most works of fiction and numerous books and articles in which vampire bats are only mentioned incidentally. Those publications consulted or quoted in the preparation of this book are indicated by an asterisk (*).

---

*ACHA, P. N., and P. V. ARAMBULO, III. 1985. Rabies in the tropics -- history and current status. *In* Rabies in the tropics, E. Kuwert, C. Mérieux, H. Koprowski, and K. Bogel, eds. Springer-Verlag, Berlin, Heidelberg, New York, and Tokyo.

*ACHA, P. N., and A. MÁLAGA ALBA. 1988. Economic losses due to *Desmodus rotundus*. *In* The natural history of vampire bats, A. M Greenhall and U. Schmidt, eds. CRC Press, Inc. Boca Raton, FL.

ALLEN, G. M. 1935. Bats from the Panama region. J. Mammal. 16:226-228.

*_____. 1939. Bats. Cambridge Univ. Press.

ALLEN, H. 1896. Notes on the vampire bat (*Diphylla ecaudata*) with special reference to its relationships with *Desmodus rufus*. Proc. U.S. Nat. Mus. 18:769-777.

*ALLEN, J. A. 1916. Mammals collected on the Roosevelt Brazilian expedition, with field notes by Leo E. Miller. Bull. Amer. Mus. Nat. Hist. 35:559-610.

*ALTENBACH, J. S. 1979. Locomotor morphology of the vampire bat, *Desmodus rotundus*. Amer. Soc. Mammalogists Spec. Publ. 6:1-137.

*ALVAREZ, T. 1963. The recent mammals of Tamaulipas, Mexico. Univ. Kansas Mus. Nat. Hist. Publ. 14:363-473.

ALVAREZ, del TORO, M. 1977. Los mamiferos de Chiapas. Univ. Autónoma de Chiapas, Tustla Gutierrez.

121

ANDERSON, S. A. 1960. Neotropical bats from western Mexico. Univ. Kansas Mus. Nat. Hist. Publ. 14:1-8.

*_____. 1972. Mammals of Chihuahua: Taxonomy and Distribution. Bull. Amer. Mus. Nat. Hist. 148:151-410.

*ANGHIERA, P. MARTYRE. 1511-1516. The decades of the new worlde or west India. Pp. 65-185 *In* E. Araber (ed.), Three English books on America. Transl. and compil. by R. Eden. Turnbull and Spears, Edinburgh, 1885.

*ANONYMOUS. 1932. Vampire bats and Panama horse disease. Science (supplement) 76(1979):8-9.

*_____. 1937. The real vampire:the little bat that has "deposed" vampyrus. London News 191(5139):653.

_____. 1946. Sanguinary sippers. Pathfinder 53(31):32.

_____. 1966. Vampire saliva prevents clotting. Science News 90:448.

_____. 1969. Vampire bat eradication. Science News 95:551.

*ARATA, A. A., J. B. VAUGHN, and M. E. THOMAS. 1967. Food habits of certain Columbian bats. J. Mammal. 48:653-655.

ARREDONDO, O. 1958. El vampiro Cubano. Rev. Scout, p. 6-7, 10.

ARRIAGA, P. J. de. 1620 (1968). The extirpation of idolatry in Peru. Trans. and edited by L. C. Keating. Univ. Kentucky Press, Lexington.

*BAER, G. M., ed. 1975. The natural history of rabies. 2 vols. Academic Press, New York.

*BAKER, R. H., and J. GREER. 1960. Notes on Oaxacan mammals. J. Mammal. 41:413-415.

_____. 1962. Mammals of the Mexican state of Durango. Publ. Michigan State Univ. Mus., Biol. Series 2:71-72.

*BAKER, R. H., and G. LÓPEZ. 1968. Notes on some bats of Tamaulipas. Southwest. Natural. 13:361-362.

BAKER, R. J., J. K. JONES, Jr., and D. C. CARTER (eds). 1976. Biology of bats of the New World Family Phyllostomatidae, Part I. Spec. Publ. Mus. Texas Tech. Univ. 10:218+.

BANG, N. V. 1991. Leeches, snakes, ticks, and vampire bats in today's cardiovascular drug development. Circul. 84:436+.

*BATES, H. W. 1863 (1892). The naturalist on the river Amazons. John Murray and Sons, London.

*BEEBE, C. W. 1925. Edge of the jungle. Garden City Publ. Co., New York.

*_____. 1927. The vampire's bite. Bull. New York Zool. Soc. 30:113-115.

*BEEBE, M. B., and C. W. BEEBE. 1910. Our search for a wilderness. Henry Holt and Co., New York.

*BELWOOD, J. J., and P. A. MORTON. Vampires: the real story. Bats (Bat Conservation International) 9:11-16.

*BENSON, E. P. 1987. Bats in South American iconography. Andean Past 1:165-190.

*_____. 1988. The Maya and the bat. Latin American Indian Literatures J. 4:99:124.

*BENZONI, M. G. 1565 (1970). History of the New World. Transl. by W. H. SMYTH. Burt Franklin, Publisher, New York.

*BERNSTEIN, J. 1952. Portrait of a vampire. Nat. Hist. 61(2):83-87, 92-94.

*BHATNAGER, K. P. 1978. Breech presentation in the hairy-legged vampire *Diphylla ecaudata*. J. Mammal. 59:864-866.

*BIRNEY, E. C. and R. M. TIMM. 1975. Dental ontogeny and adaptation in *Diphylla ecaudata*. J. Mammal. 56:204-207.

*BLAFFER, S. C. 1972. The black-man of Zinacantan. Univ. Texas Press, Austin and London.

*BLOEDEL, P. 1955. Observations on the life histories of Panama bats. J. Mammal. 36:232-235.

*BOONE, E. H. 1983. The Codex Magliabechiano. Univ. California Press, Berkeley, Los Angeles, and London.

*BRASS, D. 1993. Rabies in bats: natural history and public health implications. Livia Press, Ridgefield, CT.

*BROWN, C. B. 1876. Canoe and camp life in British Guiana. Edward Stanford, London.

*BROWN, J. H. 1968. Activity patterns of some neotropical bats. J. Mammal. 49:754-757.

BREUDEBSTEUBM C. P. 1984. The palatability of reconstituted freeze-dried blood when used as a food supply for vampire bats (*Desmodus rotundus*). Bat Res. News. 25:3.

*BULLARD, R. W., and S. A. SHUMAKE. 1973. Food temperature preference response of *Desmodus rotundus*. J. Mammal. 54:299-302.

*BULLARD, R. W., and R. D. THOMPSON. 1977. Efficacy and safety of the systemic method of vampire bat control. Interciencia 2:149-152.

*BURNS, R. J. 1970. Twin vampire bats born in captivity. J. Mammal. 51:391-392.

*BURNS, R. J., and R. W. BULLARD. 1979. Diphacinone residue from whole bodies of vampire bats: a laboratory study. Bull. Pan Amer. Health Org. 13:365-369.

*BURNS, R. J., and R. F. CRESPO. 1975. Notes on local movement and reproduction of vampire bats in Colima, Mexico. Southwest. Natural. 19:446.

*BURT, W. H. 1938. Faunal relationships and geographic distribution of mammals in Sonora, Mexico. Univ. of Mich. Zool. Misc. Publ. Zool. 39:7-77.

BURT, W. H., and R. A. STIRTON. 1961. The mammals of El Salvador. Univ. of Mich. Mus. Zool. Misc. Publ. 117:1-69.

*BURTON, R. F. 1869. The highlands of the Brazil. 2 vols. Tinsley Brothers, London.

*BURTON, R. F. 1893 (1st ed. 1870). Vikram and the vampire. Tylston and Edwards, London.

BUSCH, C. 1988. Consumption of blood, renal function and utilization of free water by the vampire bat, *Desmodus rotundus.* Comp. Biochem. Physiol. 90A:141.

BUSH, D. L. 1961. Epizootic bat rabies in Surinam. J. Amer. Vet. Med. Assoc. 138:363-365.

*BYRON, G. G. 1831. The Giaour, a fragment of / a Turkish tale. John Murray, London.

*CABEZA DE VACA, A. N. 1555. The conquest of the River Platte (1535-1555). (Translated for the Hakluyt Soc.). Burt Franklin, Publisher, New York.

CARACCIOLO, H. 1895. Bats. J. Trinidad Field Natural. Club 2:164-170.

*CARNEIRO, V. 1954. Transmission of rabies by bats in Latin America. Bull. World Health Org. 10:775-780.

*CARTER, M. L. 1988. Dracula: the vampire and the critics. UMI Research Press, Ann Arbor, MI and London.

*_____. (ed). 1989. The vampire in literature. UMI Research Press, Ann Arbor, MI and London.

CARTWRIGHT, T. 1974. The plasminogen activator of vampire bat saliva. Blood 43:317.

CARTWRIGHT, T., and C. HAWKEY. 1969. Activation of the blood fibrinolytic mechanism in birds by saliva of the vampire bat *Diaemus youngi.* J. Physiol. 201:1-45.

*CHOATE, J. R., and P. L. CLIFTON. 1970. Noteworthy records of bats from Tamaulipas, Mexico. Southwest. Natural. 14:358-360.

*CHURCHILL, A., ed. 1774. A collection of voyages and travels, some now first printed from original mss., others now first published in England. 3rd ed., 6 vols. Lintot and Osborn, London.

CLARK, H. C., and J. BENAVIEDES. 1935. The cattle reservoir for equine trypanosomiasis in Panama. Amer. J. Tropical Med. 15:285-299.

CLARK, H. C., T. L. CASSERLY, and I. O. GLADISH. 1933. Equine trypanosomiasis -- "murrina" or "derrengadera." J. Amer. Vet. Med. Assoc. 83:358-389.

COBO, B. 1653 (1979). History of the Inca Empire. Trans. and edited by R. Hamilton. Univ. Texas Press, Austin and London.

*CONSTANTINE, D. G. 1970. Bats in relation to the health, welfare, and economy of man. Pp. 319-449. *In* Biology of bats, Vol. 2, W. W. Wimsatt, ed. Academic Press, New York and London.

*CUVIER, B. 1831. Animal kingdom. 4 vols. G. & C. & H. Carville, New York.

*CUTRIGHT, P. R. 1940. The vampire bat, p. 47-57 *In* The great naturalists explore South America. The MacMillan Co., New York.

DALQUEST, W. W. 1953. Mammals of the Mexican state of San Luis Potosí. Louisiana State Univ. Press Biol. Sci. Ser. 1.

*_____. 1955. Natural history of the vampire bats of eastern Mexico. Amer. Midl. Nat. 53:79-87.

*DALQUEST, W. W., and E. R. HALL. 1947. Geographic range of the hairy-legged vampire in eastern Mexico. Trans. Kansas Acad. Sci. 50:315-317.

*DALQUEST, W. W., and H. J. WERNER. 1954. Histological aspects of the faces of North American bats. J. Mammal. 35:147.

*DARWIN, C. 1878. Journal of researches into the natural history and geology of the countries visited during the voyage of H.M.S. Beagle round the world, under the command of Capt. FitzRoy, R.N. D. Appleton and Co., New York.

*DAVIS, D. E. 1945. The home range of some Brazilian mammals. J. Mammal. 26:119-127.

*DAVIS, W. B. 1944. Notes on Mexican mammals. J. Mammal. 25:370-403.

*DAVIS, W. B., and R. J. RUSSELL, Jr. 1952. Bats of the Mexican state of Morelos. J. Mammal. 33:234-239.

*DICKEY, H. S., and D. HAWTHORE. 1929. Misadventures of a tropical medico. Dodd, Mead & Co., New York.

DICKSON, J. M., and D. G. GREEN. 1970. The vampire bat (*Desmodus rotundus*): improved methods of laboratory care and handling. Lab. Anim. 4:37+.

DiSANTO, P. E. 1960. Anatomy and histochemistry of the salivary glands of the vampire bat *Desmodus rotundus murinus*. J. Morphol. 106:301+.

*DITMARS, R. L. 1934. Confessions of a scientist. MacMillan Co., New York.

*_____. 1935. Vampire research. Bull. Zool. Soc. (New York) 38:29-31.

*_____. 1937. The making of a scientist. MacMillan Co., New York.

*_____. 1941. Vampires from Trinidad. Bull. Zool. Soc. (New York) 44:171-176.

DITMARS, R. L., and W. BRIDGES. 1935. Snake hunter's holiday. D. Appleton-Century, New York.

*DITMARS, R. L., and A. M. GREENHALL. 1935. The vampire bat -- a presentation of undescribed habits and review of its history. Zoologica 19:53-76.

*DOMVILLE-FIFE, C. W. 1924. Among wild tribes of the Amazons. Seely, Service & Co., London.

*DRESSER, N. 1989. American vampires: Fans, victims and practioners. W. W. Norton and Co., New York and London.

*DUGES, A., 1911. El vampiro de Tierra Caliente. La Naturaleza Mexico. Ser. 3, Vol. 1, No.2:1-4.

*DUGUID, J. 1931. Green hell. The Century Co., New York.

DUNN, L. H. 1932. Experiments in the transmission of *Trypanosoma hippicum* Darling, with the vampire bat, *Desmodus rotundus murinus* Wagner, as a vector in Panama. J. Prev. Med. 6:415-424.

REFERENCES

*_____. 1933. Observations on the carnivorous habits of the spear-nosed bat, *Phyllostomus hastatus panamensis* Allen, in Panama. J. Mammal. 14:188-199.

*DYOTT, G. M. 1924. Silent highways of the jungle. Chapman and Dodd, London.

*_____. 1935. Killer bats. Outdoor Life 75(6):16-17, 85, 99.

EAVES, A. O. 1904. Modern vampirism. Talisman Publ. Co., Harrogate, U.K.

*FARSON, D. 1975. Vampires, zombies, and monster men. Doubleday & Co., New York.

FANU, J. S., Le. 1872. Carmilla: In a glass darkly. Bently, London.

*FASH, W. L. 1991. Scribes, warriors and kings: the city of Copán and the ancient Maya. Thames and Hudson, London.

*FAWCETT, P. H. 1953. Lost trails, lost cities... Funk and Wagnalls, New York.

*FENTON, M. B. 1990. The origin of blood-feeding in bats. *In* 20th Ann. N. Amer. Symp. on Bat Research, Lincoln, NB.

*FIEDLER, J. 1979. Prey catching with and without echolocation in the Indian false vampire bat *Megaderma lyra*. Behav. Ecol. Sociobiol. 6:155-160.

*FITTER, M. 1968. How not to control vampire bats. Oryx 9:248-249.

*FLETCHER, J. C., and D. P. KIDDER. 1879. Brazil and the Brazilians. Little, Brown, and Co., Boston.

*FLORES-CRESPO, R., J. BURNS, and S. B. LINHART. 1970. Load-lifting capacity of the vampire bat. J. Mammal. 51:627-629.

*FLORES-CRESPO, R., S. S. FERNANDEZ, D. D. LÓPEZ, F. I. VELARDE, and R. M. ANAYA. 1979. Intramuscular inoculation of cattle with Warfarin: a new technique for control of vampire bats. Bull. Pan Amer. Health Org. 13:147-161.

*FLORES-CRESPO, R., S. B. LINHART, and R. J. BURNS. 1972. Behavior of the vampire bat (*Desmodus rotundus*) in captivity. Southwest. Natural. 17:139.

*FLORES-CRESPO, R., S. B. LINHART, R. J. BURNS, and G. C. MITCHELL. 1972. Foraging behavior of the common vampire bat related to moonlight. J. Mammal. 53:366-368.

FORMAN, G. L., R. J. BAKER, and J. D. GERBER. 1968. Comments on the systematic status of vampire bats (family Desmodontidae). Syst. Zool. 17:417-425.

*FORMENT, W. L., U. SCHMIDT, and A. M. GREENHALL. 1971. Movement and population studies of the vampire bat (*Desmodus rotundus* in Mexico. J. Mammal. 52:227-228.

*FORNES, A., R. D. LORD, M. L. KUNS, O. P. LARGHI, E. FUENZALIDA, and L. LAZARA. 1974. Control of bovine rabies through vampire bat control. J. Wildl. Dis. 10:310-316.

*FOX, L. A. 1942. Mad dogs with wings (vampire bats). U.S. Army Med. Bull. 60:122-127.

*FRAYLING, C., ed. 1978. The vampyre: a bedtime companion. Charles Scribner's Sons, New York.

*FROST, B. J. 1989. The monster with a thousand faces: guises of the vampire in myth and literature. Bowling Green State Univ. Popular Press, Bowling Green, OH. 152p.

*GADOW, H. 1908. Through southern Mexico. Witherby & Co., London.

*GANN, T. 1926. Ancient cities and modern tribes: exploration and adventure in Maya lands. Charles Scribner's Sons, New York.

GARDNER, A. L. 1977. Feeding habits. *In* Biology of bats of the New World Family Phyllostomatidae. Part II, R. J. Baker, J. K. Jones, Jr, and D. C. Carter, eds. Spec. Publ. Mus. Texas Tech 13:1-293.

*GARDNER, A. L., R. K. LaVAL, and D. E. WILSON. 1970. The distributional status of some Costa Rican bats. J. Mammal. 51:712-729.

*GARDNER, G. 1849. Travels in the interior of Brazil. Reeve, Benham, and Reeve, London.

*GENOWAYS, H. H., and J. K. JONES, Jr. 1968. Notes on bats from the Mexican state of Zacatecas. J. Mammal. 49:743-745.

*GLUT, D. F., 1975. The Dracula book. Scarecrow Press, Inc., Metuchen, NJ.

GOLDMAN, E. A. 1920. Mammals of Panama. Smithsonian Misc. Coll. 69:1-309.

*GOODMAN, E. J. 1972. The explorers of South America. Univ. of Oklahoma Press, Norman.

*GOODWIN, G. G. 1928. Flying shadows of the night. Nat. Hist. 28:515-522.

_____. 1934. Mammals collected by A. W. Anthony in Guatemala, 1924-1928. Bull. Amer. Mus. Nat. Hist. 141:1-270.

*GOODWIN, G. G., and A. M. GREENHALL. 1961. A review of the bats of Trinidad and Tobago. Bull. Amer. Mus. Nat. Hist. 122:187-302.

*GOTCH, A. F. 1979. Mammals -- their Latin names explained: a guide to animal classifications. Blandford Press, Poole and Dorset, UK. 271p

*GREENHALL, A. M. 1952. Profile of a vampire. Pageant 8(6):52-57.

*_____. 1959. The ecological role of Trinidad's bats, especially the vampire, and bat rabies. Vet. Record 71:188-190.

*_____. 1963. Use of mist nets and strychnine for vampire control in Trinidad. J. Mammal. 44:396-399.

_____. 1965. Notes on the behavior of captive vampire bats. Mammalia 29:441-451.

*_____. 1965. Trinidad and bat research. Nat. Hist. 74(6):14-21.

_____. 1968. Bats, rabies and control problems. Oryx 9:263.

_____. 1968. Problems and ecological implications in the control of vampire bats. Intern. Union for the Conserv. of Nature, New Series Publ. 13:94-102.

_____. 1970. The use of a precipitin test to determine host preferences of the vampire bats, *Desmodus rotundus* and *Diaemus youngi*. Bijdragen tot de Dierkunde 40:36-39.

127

_____. 1970. Vampire bat control: a review and proposed research programme for Latin America. Proced. Vert. Pest Conf., Berkeley, CA 4:41-54.

*_____. 1972. The biting and feeding habits of the vampire bat, *Desmodus rotundus*. J. Zool., London 168:451-461.

*_____. 1972. The problem of bat rabies, migratory bats, livestock and wildlife. Trans. No. Amer. Wildl. and Nat. Resour. Conf. 37:287-293.

*_____. 1972. Identification of the vampire bat. Wild Animal Rev. (FAO). 2:44+.

_____. 1986. Care in captivity [*Desmodus rotundus*]. *In* Biology of bats of the New World family Phyllostomatidae. I. R. J. Baker, J. K. Jones, and D. C. Carter, eds. Spec. Publ. Mus. Texas Tech Univ. 10:89+..

*_____. Feeding behavior. 1988. *In* The natural history of the vampire bat, A. M. Greenhall and U. Schmidt, eds. CRC Press, Inc., Boca Raton, FL.

*GREENHALL, A. M., G. JOERMANN, U. SCHMIDT, and M. R. SEIDEL. 1983. *Desmodus rotundus*. *In* Mammalian Species. Amer. Soc. Mammal. 202:1-6.

*GREENHALL, A. M., and U. SCHMIDT (eds.). 1988. Natural history of vampire bats. CRC Press, Inc., Boca Raton, FL.

*GREENHALL, A. M., U. SCHMIDT, and G. JOERMANN. 1984. *Diphylla ecaudata*. *In* Mammalian Species. Amer. Soc. Mammal. 227:1-3.

*GREENHALL, A. M., U. SCHMIDT, and W. LOPEZ-FORMENT. 1971. Attacking behavior of the vampire bat, *Desmodus rotundus*, under field conditions in Mexico. Biotropica 3(2):136-141.

GRIFFIN, D. R., and A. NOVICK. 1955. Acoustic orientation in neotropical bats. J. Exp. Zool. 130:251-300.

*GUENTHER, K. 1931. A naturalist in Brazil. Translated by B. Miall. Houghton Mifflin Co., Boston and New York.

*GUISE, A. V. L. 1922. Six years in Bolivia. T. Fisher Unwin, London.

GULLION, A. 1910. Les vampires. Clinique (Paris) 5:433-436.

*GUT, H. J. 1959. A pleistocene vampire bat from Florida. J. Mammal. 40:534-538.

GUTHRIE, D. A. 1980. Analysis of avifaunal and bat remains from a midden site on San Miguel Island. Pp. 689-702 *In* The California Islands: proceedings of a multidisciplinary Symposium, D. M. Power, ed. Santa Barbara Mus. Nat. Hist., CA.

*HAGEN, V. W., von. 1945. South America called them. Alfred A. Knopf, New York.

*HALL, E. R. 1981. The mammals of North America, 2nd ed. John Wiley and Sons, New York. Vol. 1.

*HALL, E. R., and W. W. DALQUEST. 1963. Mammals of Vera Cruz, Mexico. Univ. Kansas Mus. Nat. Hist. Publ. 14(14):165-362.

HAMILTON, A. 1973. Vampire bat: rabies on wings of night. Sci. Dig. 73 (Mar):16-21.

*HANSON, E. P. 1938. Journey to Manáos. Reynal and Hitchcock, New York.

*HATT, R. T. 1938. Notes concerning mammals collected in Yucatán. J. Mammal. 19:333-337.

*HAWKEY, C. M. 1966. Plasminogen activator in saliva of the vampire bat *Desmodus rotundus*). Nature (London) 211:434-435.

*HEICK, A. 1992. Prince Dracula, rabies, and the vampire legend. Ann. Int. Med. 117:172-173.

*HEMPHILL, R. E., and T. ZABOW. 1983. Clinical vampirism. S. Africa Med. J. 63:278-281.

*HERNDON, W. L., and L. GIBBON. 1854. Exploration of the Valley of the Amazon made under direction of the Navy Department. Robert Armstrong, Wash. D. C.

*HERRERA, A. L. 1911. Nota adicional. La Naturaleza de Mexico. Sr. 3(1), No. 2:4-6.

*HILL, J. E., and J. D. SMITH. 1984. Bats: a natural history. Univ. Texas Press, Austin. 243p.

*HINGSTON, R. W. G. 1932. A naturalist in the Guiana forest. Edward Arnold & Co., London.

*HOARE, C. A. 1965. Vampire bats as vectors and hosts of equine and bovine trypanosomes. Acta Tropica 22:204-216.

HONEYCUTT, R. L., I. F. GREENBAUN, R. J. BAKER, and V. M. SARICH. 1981. Molecular evolution of vampire bats. J. Mammal. 62:805-814.

*HORST, R., and M. LANGWORTHY. 1972. Rabies in a colony of vampire bats. J. Mammal. 53:903-905.

*HOYT, R. A., and J. S. ALTENBACH. 1981. Observations on *Diphylla ecaudata* in captivity. J. Mammal. 62:215-216.

*HUMBOLDT, A., von, and A. BONPLAND. 1852. A personal narrative of travels to the equinoctial regions of America. Trans. and ed. by Thomasina Ross. 3 vols. Henry G. Bohn, London.

*HURST, E. W., and J. L. PAWAN. 1931. An outbreak of rabies in Trinidad. Lancet 2:622-628.

*HUSSON, A. M. 1962. The bats of Suriname. E. J. Brill, Leiden. p. 282.

HUXLEY, T. H. 1865. On the structure in *Desmodus rufus*. Proc. Zool. Soc. London. 22:386-390.

*ImTHURN, E. F. 1883. Among the Indians of Guiana. Kegan, Paul, Trench & Co., London.

*INSKIPP, T. and J. BARZDO. 1987. World checklist of threatened mammals. Nature Conservancy Council, UK.

JOERMANN, G., and U. SCHMIDT. 1980. Obstacle avoidance in the common vampire bat *Desmodus rotundus*. Myotis. 18/19:142.

*JOHNSON, H. N. 1948. Derriengue: vampire bat rabies in Mexico. Amer. J. Hyg. 47:189-204.

129

JONES, J. K., Jr. 1958. Bats from Guatemala. Univ. Kansas Publ., Mus. Nat. Hist. 16:439-472.

*KING, B. G., and R. SAPHIR. 1937. Some observations on the feeding methods of the vampire bat. Zoologica:22:281-287.

*KIRKE, H. 1898. Twenty-five years in British Guiana. Sampson, Low, Marston, and Co., London.

*KÖHLER, U. 1985. The flying blackman in Highland Chiapas and beyond. Latin American Indian Literatures J. 1:122-136.

*KOOPMAN, K. F. 1958. A fossil vampire bat from Cuba. Breviora 90:1-5.

*_____. 1958. Land bridges and ecology in bat distribution on islands off the northern coast of South America. Evol. 12:429-439.

*_____. 1961. A collection of bats from Sinaloa, with remarks on the limits of the neotropical region in northwestern Mexico. J. Mammal. 42:536-538.

*_____. 1988. Systematics and distribution. *In* The natural history of vampire bats. A. M. Greenhall and U. Schmidt, eds. CRC Press, Inc., Boca Raton, FL.

*KRAVIGNY, F. W. 1911. The jungle route. Orlin Tremaine, New York.

KUMM, H. W. 1932. Yellow fever transmission experiments with South American bats. Ann. Trop. Med. and Parisit. 26:207-213.

*KUNS, M. L., and R. E. TASHIAN. 1954. Notes on mammals from northern Chiapas, Mexico. J. Mammal. 35:100-103.

*KURTEN, B., and E. ANDERSON. 1980. Pleistocene mammals of North America. Columbia Univ. Press, NY. 442p.

*KURTEN, L., and U. SCHMIDT. 1982. Thermoperception in the common vampire bat (*Desmodus rotundus*). J. Comp. Physiol. 146:223-228.

*KUWERT, E., C. MÉRIEUX, H. KOPROWSKI, and K. BOGEL, eds. 1985. Rabies in the tropics. Springer-Verlag, Berlin, Heidelberg, New York, and Tokyo.

*KVERNO, N. B., and G. C. MITCHELL. 1976. Vampire bats and their effect on cattle production in Latin America. World Anim. Rev. (FAO) 17:1-7.

*LACKEY, J. A. 1970. Distributional records of bats from VeraCruz. J. Mammal. 51:384-385.

*La CONDAMINE, C. M. 1745. Relation abrégeé d'un voyage fait dans l'intérieur de l'Amerique méridionale, depuis la cote de la mer du sud, jufques aux côtes du Bréfil & de la Guiane, en defcendant la rivierè des Amazones. Mém. Acad. Roy. Sci. (Paris), p. 391-429.

La TORRE, L., de, and D. E. BEDFORD. 1964. The microanatomy of the tongue of the vampire bat. Bat Research News 5:32.

*La VAL, R. K. 1970. Banding returns and activity periods of some Costa Rican bats. Southwest. Natural. 15:1-10.

*LAWLOR, T. E. 1973. Aerodynamic characteristics of some Neotropical bats. J. Mammal. 54:71-78.

LAYCOCK, G. 1978. Abajo los vampiros: new ways to combat losses from vampire bats. Audubon Mag. 80(Mar.):107.

*LÉVI-STRAUS, C. 1969. The raw and the cooked. Transl. by J. and D. Weightman. Harper and Row, New York and Evanston.

*LEWIN, R. 1986. Why dynamiting vampire bats is wrong. Science 232:24-26.

*LEWIS, W. C. 1990. Airborne rabies in bat maternity caves. NSS News, Nov.:282-286.

*LINHART, S. B. 1971. A partial bibliography of the vampire bats *Desmodus, Diphylla, Diaemus*. U.S. Bur. Sport Fish. and Wildl., Denver Wildl. Res. Center.

*_____. 1973. Age determination and occurrence of incremental growth lines in the dental cementum of the common vampire bat (*Desmodus rotundus*). J. Mammal. 54:493-496.

_____. 1975. The biology and control of vampire bats. p. 221-241 *In* The natural history of rabies (G. M. Baer, ed.). Academic Press, New York.

LINHART, S. B., R. FLORES-CRESPO, and G. C. MITCHELL. 1972. Control of vampire bats by topical application of an anticoagulant, chlorophacinone. Bull. Pan Amer. Health Org. 6:31+.

*LINNAEUS, C. 1758. Systema naturae. Regnum animale, ed. 10, vol. 1. Holmiae.

*LOOMIS, R. B., and R. M. DAVIS. 1965. The vampire bat in Sonora, with notes on other bats from southern Sonora. J. Mammal. 46:497.

*LOPEZ, R., P. MIRANDA, V. TEJADA, and D. B. FISHBEIN. 1992. Outbreak of human rabies in the Peruvian jungle. Lancet 339:408-411.

LOPEZ-FORMENT, W. 1980. Longevity of wild *Desmodus rotundus* in Mexico. *In* Proc. of the 5th Intern. Bat Research Conf., A. L. Gardner, ed. Texas Tech Press, Lubbock.

*LOPEZ-FORMENT, W., U. SCHMIDT, and A. M. GREENHALL. 1971. Movement and population studies of the vampire bat (*Desmodus rotundus*) in Mexico. J. Mammal. 52:227-228.

LORD, R. D. 1971. A simple inexpensive cage for vampire bats. Zoonosis 13:225.

_____. 1980. An ecological strategy for controlling rabies through elimination of vampire bats. Proc. Vert. Pest Conf. 9:4.

*_____. 1992. Seasonal reproduction of vampire bats and its relation to seasonality of bovine rabies. J. Wildl. Dis. 28:292-294.

*LORD, R. D., E. FUENZALIDA, H. DELPIETRO, O. P. LARGHI, A. M. O. DÍAZ, and L. LAZÁRO. 1975. Observations on the epizootiology of vampire bat rabies. Bull. Pan Amer. Health Org. 9:189-195.

*LORD, R. D., F. MURADALI, and L. LAZÁRO. 1976. Age composition of vampire (*Desmodus rotundus*) bats in northern Argentina and southern Brazil. J. Mammal. 57:573-576.

*LOVE, B. B. 1992. The encyclopedia of unusual sex practices. Barricade Books, Inc., Fort Lee, NJ.

*LUKENS, P. W., Jr., and W. B. DAVIS. 1957. Bats of the Mexican state of Guerrero. J. Mammal. 38:1-14.

*LYDEKKER, R. 1893. The royal natural history. 6 vols. Frederick Warne & Co., London.

*LYMAN, C. P., and W. A. WIMSATT. 1966. Temperature regulation in the vampire bat, *Desmodus rotundus*. Physiol. Zool. 39::101-109.

*LYON, H. W., Jr. 1931. The vampire bat. Science 73(1883):124-125.

MacCULLOCH, C. J. A. 1932. The mythology of all races. 13 vols. Archeological Instit. of Amer., Marshall Jones Co., Boston.

MALÁGA-ALBA, A. 1954. Vampire bat as a carrier of rabies. Amer. J. Pub. Health 44:909.

*_____. 1957. Rabies in wildlife in Middle America. J. Amer. Vet. Med. Assoc. 130:386-342.

MANSKE, U., and U. SCHMIDT. 1976. Visual acuity of the vampire bat, *Desmodus rotundus*, and its dependence upon light intensity. Z. Tierpsychol. 42:215-221.

*MARES, M. A., and D. J. SCHMIDLY (eds). 1991. Latin American mammalogy. Univ. Oklahoma Press, Norman.

*MARTIN, M., and P. S. MARTIN. 1954. Notes on the capture of tropical bats at Cuevo El Pachon, Tamaulipas, Mexico. J. Mammal. 35:584-585.

MARTIN, R. A. 1972. Synopsis of late Pliocene and Pleistocene bats of North America and the Antilles. Amer. Midl. Natural. 87:326-335.

*MASCETTI, M. D. 1992. Vampire: The complete guide to the world of the undead. Penguin Books Ltd., London.

MASTERS, A. 1972. The natural history of the vampire. G. P. Putnam's Sons, New York.

MATHESON, R. Drink my red blood. Imagination 2 (April).

*McCARTHY, C. 1985. Blood meridian. Vintage Books (Random House, Inc.), New York.

*McCARTHY, T. J. 1989. Human depredation by vampire bats (*Desmodus rotundus*) following a hog cholera campaign. Amer. J. Trop. Med. Hyg. 40:320-322.

McFARLAND, W. N., and W. A. WIMSATT. 1969. Renal function and its relation to the ecology of the vampire bat, Desmodus rotundus. Comp. Biochem. Physiol. 28:985-1006.

*McGOVERN, W. M. 1927. Jungle paths and Inca ruins. Hutchinson & Co., London.

McKENDRICK, A. G. 1935. Rabies: a review of recent articles. Trop. Dis. Bull. 32:605.

*McNAB, B. K. 1973. Energetics and the distribution of vampires. J. Mammal. 54:131-144.

*McNALLY, R. T., and R. FLORESCU. 1972. In search of Dracula. New York Graphic Soc., Greenwich, CT.

*MEDELLÍN, R. A. 1988. Prey of *Chrotopterus auritus*, with notes on feeding behavior. J. Mammal. 69:841-844.

*MILLER, L. E. 1918. In the wilds of South America. Charles Scribner's Sons, New York.

*MILLS, D. 1931. The country of the Orinoco. Hutchinson and Co., London.

*MILLS, R. S. 1980. Parturition and social interaction among captive vampire bats, *Desmodus rotundus*. J. Mammal. 61:336-337.

*MITCHELL, G. C., 1986. Vampire bat control in Latin America. p. 151-164, *In* Ecological knowledge and environmental problem-solving. National Acad. Press, Washington, D. C.

*MITCHELL, G. C., and R. J. BURNS. 1973. Chemical control of vampire bats. U.S. Bur. Sports Fisheries and Wildlife, Denver.

MITCHELL, G. C., R. J. BURNS, and A. L. KOLZ. 1973. Rastreo del comportamiento nocturno de los murciélagos vampiros por radiotelemetria. Tecnica Pecuaria en Mexico 24:47.

*MITCHELL, G. C., and J. R. TIGNER. 1970. The route of ingested blood in the vampire bat (*Desmodus rotundus*). J. Mammal. 51:814-817.

MOHR, C. E. 1948. What about vampire bats? The caves of Texas. Bull. Nat. Speleol. Soc. 10:106-107.

*_____. 1955. Cave of the vampires. Pp. 39-58. *In* Celebrated American caves (C. E. Mohr and H. N. Sloan, eds.), Rutgers Univ. Press, NJ.

*MOLINA SOLÍS, J. F. 1896. Historia del descubrimiento y conquista de Yucatán, con una reseña de la historia antiqua de la península. Mérida.

*MONDEY, D. 1982. The Hamlyn concise guide to American aircraft of World War II. Hamlyn/Aerospace, London, New York, Sydney, Toronto.

*MONTAÑO, J. A., G. W. POLACK, and E. F. MORA. 1988. Rabies in vaccinated cattle. II. Epidemiological situation in the state of Parana, Brazil -- 1984. Vet. Bull. 58:18.

*MORENO, J. A., and G. M. BAER. 1980. Experimental rabies in the vampire bat. Amer. J. Trop. Med. Hyg. 29:254-259.

*MOZANS, H. J. (J. A. ZAHM). 1911. Along the Andes and down the Amazon. D. Appleton & Co., New York.

*_____. 1916. Through South America's southland. D. Appleton & Co., New York.

*MURPHY, M. J. 1979. The celluloid vampires: a history and filmography, 1897-1979. Pierian Press, Ann Arbor, MI.

*MURPHY, R. C. 1925. Bird islands of Peru. C. R. Putnam's Sons, New York.

*MYERS, H. M., and P. V. N. 1871. Life and nature under the tropics. D. Appleton and Co., New York.

*MYERS, P., and R. M. WETZEL. 1983. Systematics and zoogeography of the bats of the Chaco Boreal. Misc. Publ. Mus. Zool. Univ. Michigan 165:1-59.

*NAVARRO-L., D., 1979. *Vampyrum spectrum* (Chiroptera, Phyllostomatidae) in Mexico. J. Mammal. 60:435.

133

*NEHAUL, B. B. G. 1955. Rabies transmitted by bats in British Guiana. Amer. J. Trop. Med. Hyg. 4:550-553.

*NEHAUL, B. B. G., and A. E. DYRTING. 1965. An outbreak of rabies in man in British Guiana. Amer. J. Trop. Med. Hyg. 14:295-296.

*NESBITT, L. M. 1936. Desolate marches. Harcourt Brace & Co., New York.

*NOLL, R. 1992. Vampires, werewolves and demons. Brunner/Mazel, New York.

*NORWOOD, V. G. C. 1964. Jungle life in Guiana. Robert Hale, London.

*NOVICK, A. 1963. Orientation in neotropical bats. II. Phyllostomatidae and Desmodontidae. J. Mammal. 44:44-56.

*NOVICK, A., and N. LEEN. 1969. The world of bats. Holt, Rinehart and Winston Publ. Co., New York, Chicago, San Francisco.

*NUTINI, H. G., and J. M. ROBERTS. 1993. Bloodsucking witchcraft. Univ. Arizona Press, Tucson and London.

*OLSEN, S. J. 1960. Additional remains of Florida's pleistocene vampire. J. Mammal. 41:458-462.

*ORTEGA, J. R. V., M. A. M. DELGADO, D. B. CAMPERO, and D. O. CORDOVA. 1987. Presence of rabies antibodies and virus in *Desmodus rotundus* and other bats in a region of the humid zone of the Tehuantepec Isthmus, Mexico. Vet. Bull. 57:283.

*ORTON, J. 1875. The Andes and the Amazon. Harper & Brothers, New York.

*OVIEDO Y VALDES, F., de. 1526 (1950). Sumario de la natural historia de las Indias. Fondo de Cultura Economica, Mexico.

PARK, H., and E. R. HALL. 1951. The gross anatomy of the tongues and stomachs of eight New World bats. Trans. Kansas Acad. Sci. 54:64.

*PAWAN, J. L. 1936. Rabies in the vampire bat of Trinidad, with special reference to the clinical course and the latency of infection. Ann. Trop. Med. Parasit. 30:401-422.

——————————. 1948. Fruit-eating bats and paralytic rabies in Trinidad. Ann. Trop. Med. Parisit. 33:21+.

*PERKOWSKI, J. L. 1976. Vampires of the Slavs. Slavica Publishers, Cambridge, MA.

PETERSON, R. 1964. Silently by night. McGraw-Hill, New York.

*PETERSON, R. L., and P. KIRMSE. 1969. Notes on *Vampyrum spectrum*, the false vampire bat in Panama. Canadian J. Zool. 47:140-142.

*PFEFFERKORN, I. 1989. Sonora: a description of the province. Trans. by T. E. Treutlein. Univ. Ariz. Press, Tucson.

*POLIDORI, J. W. 1819. The vampyre: a tale. New Monthly Mag., London, and E. E. Hosford, New York.

*PRICE, W. 1950. The mystery of the vampire bat. Nature Mag. 43:176-179.

*PRIETO, J. F., and G. M. BAER. 1972. An outbreak of bovine rabies in Tuxtepec, Oaxaca, Mexico. Amer. J. Trop. Med. Hyg. 21:219-225.

*PRINGLE, L. 1982. Vampire bats. William Morrow and Co., New York.

QUELCH, J. J. 1892. The bats of British Guiana. Timehri (New Series) 6:91-109.

*QUICK, C. R. 1975. Notes on the maintenance of the Mexican vampire bat *Desmodus rotundus murinus* at the Houston zoo. Intern. Zoo Yearbook 15:193-194.

QUINTERO, R., and J. J. RASWEILER IV. 1973. The reproductive biology of the female vampire bat, *Desmodus rotundus*. Amer. Soc. Zool. 13:1284+.

_____. 1974. Ovulation and early embryonic development in the captive vampire bat, *Desmodus rotundus*. J. Reprod. Fert. 41:265-273.

RANFT, J. L. 1974. Vampire bats. Americas 26:32-35.

RASWEILER, J. J., IV. 1979. Early embryonic development and implantation in bats. J. Reprod. Fert. 56:403+.

*RAY, C. E., O. J. LINARES, and G. S. MORGAN. 1988. Paleontology. Pp. 19-30. *In* A. M. Greenhall and U. Schmidt (eds). Natural history of vampire bats. CRC Press, Inc. Boca Raton, FL.

*REDDELL, J. R. 1968. The hairy-legged vampire, *Diphylla ecaudata*, in Texas. J. Mammal. 49:769.

*REDFORD, K. H., and J. F. EISENBERG. 1989. Mammals of the Neotropics. Two vols. Univ. Chicago Press.

REICHEL-DOLMATOFF, G. 1971. Amazonian cosmos: the sexual and religious symbolism of the Tukano Indians. Univ. Chicago Press.

*RICCARDO, M. V. 1983. Vampires unearthed -- the complete multimedia vampire and Dracula bibliography. Garland Publ., Inc., New York and London.

*RICK, A. M. 1968. Notes on bats from Tikal, Guatemala. J. Mammal. 49:516-520.

*RODITI, E. 1972. The delights of Turkey. New Directions Publ. Co., New York.

ROE, P. G. 1987. Impossible marriages. Cashi Yochiman ainbo piqui (The vampire spirit who ate a woman) and other animal seduction tales among the Shipibo Indians of the Peruvian jungle. Paper presented at the 5th Intern. Sympl on Latin American Indian Literatures, Ithaca, NY.

*ROOSEVELT, T. 1919. Through the Brazilian wilderness. Charles Scribners' Sons, New York.

*ROTH, W. E. 1915. An inquiry into the animism and folk-lore of the Guiana Indians. Ann. Rep. U.S. Bur. Ethnol. 30:103-386.

*_____. 1924. An introductory study of the arts, crafts, and customs of the Guiana Indians. Ann. Rep. U.S. Bur. Ethnol. 38:25-745.

ROUK, C. S., and B. P. GLASS. 1970. Comparative gastric histology of five North and Central American bats. J. Mammal. 51:455-472.

*RUPPRECHT, C., R. D. LORD, S. PAPO, B. DIETZSCHOLD, and A. M. GREENHALL. 1987. Bovine paralytic rabies control: immunization of vampire bats with an inactivated oral rabies vaccine. Abstract at 17th Ann. N. Amer. Symp. on Bat Research, Toronto Canada.

*RUTHVEN, A. G. 1922. The amphibians and reptiles of the Sierra Nevada de Santa Marta, Colombia. Misc. Publ. Mus. Zool., Univ. Mich. 8:1-69.

*RYAN, A., ed. 1987. Vampires: two centuries of great vampire stories. Doubleday, Garden City, NY.

*RYMER, J. M. or T. P. PREST. 1847 (1972). Varney the vampyre or, the feast of blood. E. Lloyd, London (Dover Publ., Inc., New York).

*SANBORN, C. C. 1931. Protection against vampire bats. J. Mammal. 12:312-313.

*_____. 1949. Mammals from Rio Ucayali, Peru. J. Mammal. 30:277-288.

*SANDEMAN, C. 1939. A forgotten river. Oxford Univ. Press, London, New York, and Toronto.

*SAVAGE-LANDOR, A. H. 1913. Across unknown South America. Little, Brown, & Co.

*SAZIMA, I., W. UIEDA. 1980 Feeding behavior of the white-winged vampire, *Diaemus youngii* on poultry. J. Mammal. 61:102-104.

*SCHMIDLY, D. J. 1991. The bats of Texas. Texas A&M Univ. Press, College Station.

SCHMIDT, U. 1972. Social calls of juvenile vampire bats, (Desmodus rotundus) and their mothers. Bonn. Zool. Beitr. 23:310

_____. 1973. Olfactory threshold and odor discrimination of the vampire bat (Desmodus rotundus). Period. Biol. 75:89-92.

*SCHMIDT, U., and A. M. GREENHALL. 1972. Preliminary studies of the interactions between feeding vampire bats, *Desmodus rotundus*, under natural and laboratory conditions. Mammalia 36:241-246.

SCHMIDT, U., A. M. GREENHALL, and W. LOPEZ-FORMENT. 1970. Vampire bat control in Mexico. Bijdragen Dierkunde 40:74-76.

SCHMIDT, U., and C. SCHMIDT. 1977. Echolocation performance of the vampire bat *Desmodus rotundus*. Z. Tierpsychol. 45:349-358.

SCHMIDT, U., C. SCHMIDT, W. LOPEZ-FORMENT, and R. F. CRESPO. 1978. Banding experiment on vampire bats (*Desmodus rotundus*) in Mexico. Z. Saugetierkd 43:70+.

SCHMIDT, C., U. C. SCHMIDT and U. MANSKE. 1980. Observations of the behavior of orphaned juveniles in the common vampire bat (*Desmodus rotundus*). Pp. 105-111 *In* Proc. 5th Intl. Bat Conf., Texas Tech. Press, Lubbock.

*SCHOBER, W. 1984. The lives of bats. Arco Publ., Inc., New York.

*SCHOMBURGK, R. 1922. Travels in British Guiana, 1840-1844 (Trans. and edited by W. E. Roth). 2 vols. Daily Chronicle Office, Georgetown.

*SENF, C. A. 1988. The vampire in nineteenth-century English literature. Popular Press, Bowling Green State Univ., OH.

*SENN, H. A. 1982. Were-wolf and vampire in Romania. East European Monogr., Boulder, CO. (Distr. by Columbia Univ. Press, New York).

*SHAW, G. 1800. General Zoology or systematic natural history. Mammalia, vol. 1. G. Kearsley, London.

*SHEPAARD, L., ed. 1977. The Dracula book of great vampire stories. Citadel Press, Secaucus, NJ.

*SIMPSON, G. G. 1980. Splendid isolation: the curious history of South American mammals. Yale Univ. Press, New Haven, CN.

*SIMSON, A. 1886. Travels in the wilds of Ecuador. Sampson Low, Marston, Searle, and Rivington, London.

SMITH, J. D., and H. M. GENOWAYS. 1974. Bats of Margarita Island, Venezuela, with zoogeographic comments. Bull. Southern Calif. Acad. Sciences 73:64.

*SMITH, M. C. 1977. Nightwing. W. W. Norton, New York.

*SPRUCE, R. 1908. Notes of a botanist on the Amazon and Andes. Edited and condensed by A. R. Wallace. 2 vols. Macmillan & Co., London.

*STADEN, H. 1928. The true story of his captivity. Trans. and edited by M. Letts. Robert M. McBride and Co., New York.

*STEBBINGS, R. E. 1970. Bats in danger. Oryx 10:311-312.

*STOKER, B. 1897. Dracula. Doubleday Doran & Co., Inc. Garden City, NY.

*STRUHSAKER, T. T. 1961. Morphological factors regulating flight in bats. J. Mammal. 42:152-159.

*STUART, H. V. 1891. Adventures amidst the equatorial forests and rivers of South America. John Murray, London.

*SUMNERS, M. 1928. The vampire: his kith and kin. George Routledge and Sons, Ltd., London.

* _____. 1929. The vampire in Europe. E. P. Dutton and Co., New York.

SUTHERS, R. A. 1966. Optomotor responses by echolocating bats. Science 152:1102-1104.

_____. 1970. Vision, olfaction, taste. Pp. 265-309 *In* Biology of bats, W. A. Wimsatt, ed. Academic Press, New York, Vol. 2.

SWAINSON, W. 1835. On the natural history and classification of quadrupeds. Longman, Rees, Orme, Brown, Green and Longman, London.

*SWAN, M. 1958. The marches of El Dorado. Beacon Hill Press, Boston.

TAMSITT, J. R., and I. FOX. 1970. Records of bat ectoparasites from the Caribbean region (Siphonaptera, Acarina, Diptera). Canad. J. Zool. 48:1093-1097.

*TAMSITT, J. R., and D. VALDIVIESO. 1962. *Desmodus rotundus* from a high altitude in southern Colombia. J. Mammal. 43:106-107.

* _____. 1963. Records and observations on Colombian bats. J. Mammal. 44:168-180.

*TATE, G. H. H. 1931. Random observations on habits of South American mammals. J. Mammal. 12:248-256.

*THOMAS, J. G., and H. J. HARLAN. 1981. Vampire bat bites seen in humans in Panama: their characterization, recognition and management. Military Med. 146:410-412.

*THOMPSON, J. E. S. 1966. Maya hieroglyphs of the bat as metaphorgrams. Man 1(2):176-184.

*THOMPSON, R. D., D. J. ELIAS, and G. C. MITCHELL. 1977. Effects of vampire bat control on bovine milk production. J. Wildl. Manage. 41:736-739.

THOMPSON, R. D., D. J. ELIAS, S. A. SHUMAKE, and S. E. GADDIS. 1982. Taste preferences of the common vampire bat *Desmodus rotundus*. J. Chem. Ecol. 8:715.

*THOMPSON, R. D., G. C. MITCHELL, and R. J. BURNS. 1972. Vampire bat control by systemic treatment of livestock with an anticoagulant. Science 177:806-808.

*THORNTON, H. 1980. An ingenious method of destroying the vampire bats which transmit rabies to cattle. Central African J. Med. 26:207-209.

TOWNSEND, C. H. 1927. The bite of the vampire. N. Y. Zool. Soc. Bull: 30:64-66.

*TRAPIDO, H. 1946. Observations on the vampire bat with special reference to longevity in captivity. J. Mammal. 27:217-219.

*TROUGHTON, E. 1940-41. Vampire bats in fact and legend. Australian Mus. Mag. (Sydney) 7(7):244-248.

*TSCHUDI, J. J., von. 1847. Travels in Peru. Trans. by Thomasina Ross. David Bogue, London.

*TURNER, D. C. 1975. The vampire bat -- a field study in behavior and ecology. John Hopkins Univ. Press, Baltimore and London. 145p.

TUTTLE, M. D. 1970. Distribution and zoogeography of Peruvian bats, with comments on natural history. Univ. Kansas Sci. Bull. 49:45-86.

*TWITCHELL, J. B. 1981. The living dead: a study of the vampire in romantic literature. Duke Univ. Press, Durham, NC.

*ULLOA, A.,de, and J. J. Van Y Santacilla. 1772. A voyage to South America. 2 vols. Lockyer Davis, London.

*UPDeGRAFF, F. W. 1923. Head hunters of the Amazon. Garden City Publ. Co., Inc., Garden City, NY.

*URSINI, J., and A. SILVER. 1975. The vampire film. A. S. Barnes and Co., South Brunswick and New York; Tantivy Press, London.

VALDES ORNELAS, O., and G. ATRISTAIN ARNALDE. 1964. Bat rabies in Mexico. Southern Vet. 1:13-16.

*VALDEZ, R., and R. K. LaVAL. 1971. Records of bats from Honduras and Nicaragua. J. Mammal. 52:247-250.

VATSYAYANA. (M. de Smedt, ed.). 1980. The Kama-sutra. Crown Publ., New York.

*VERLINDE, J. D., P. KOOIJ, and J. VERSTEEG. 1970. Vampire-bat transmitted rabies virus from Surinam. Trop. Geogr. Med. 22:119-122.

VERNON, J., and E. PETERSON. 1966. Hearing in the vampire bat, *Desmodus rotundus murinus*, as shown by cochlear potentials. J. Audit. Res. 6:181-187.

*VERRILL, A. H. 1929. Thirty years in the jungle. John Lane, Bodley Head Ltd., London.

*VERTEUIL, E., de, and F. W. URICH. 1936. The study and control of paralytic rabies transmitted by bats in Trinidad, British West Indies. Trans. R. Soc. Trop. Med. Hyg. 29:317-354.

*VILLA-R., B. 1961. The Mexican blood drinkers. Nat. Hist. Mag. 70(7):62-63.

*_____. 1966. Los Murciélagos de México. Instituto de Biología, Univ. Nation. Autónoma de México, México D.F.

_____. 1968. Ethology and ecology of vampire bats. Intern. Union for the Conserv. of Nature Publ., New Series 13:104-110.

_____. 1969. The ecology and biology of vampire bats and their relationship to paralytic rabies. Report to the Govern. of Brazil, No. TA2656. U.N. Devel. Programme/Food and Aquaculture Org., Rome.

VILLA-R, B., and W. LOPEZ-FORMENT. 1966. Cinco casos de depredación de pequeños verebrados en murciélagos de México. Anales Ist. Biologiá 37:187-193.

*VOLTA, O. 1965. The vampire. Tandem, London.

*WALKER, E. P., F. WARNICK, K. I. LANGE, H. E. UIBLE, S. E. HAMLET, M. A. DAVIS, and P. F. Wright. 1964. Mammals of the World. Vol. 1. John Hopkins Press, Baltimore MD.

*WALLACE, A. R. 1853. A narrative of travels on the Amazon and Rio Negro. Reeve & Co., London.

_____. 1878. Tropical nature. MacMillan & Co., London.

*WALLER, G. A. 1986. The living and the undead: from Stoker's *Dracula* to Romero's *Dawn of the Dead*. Univ. of Illinois Press, Urbana.

*WALSH, R. 1830. Notices of Brazil in 1828 and 1829. Vol. 2. Frederick Westley and A. H. Davis, London.

WATERHOUSE, G. R. 1839. The zoology of the voyage of H.M.S. Beagle. Part 2. Mammalia. Smith Elder & Co., London.

*WATERMAN, J. A. 1959. The history of the outbreak of paralytic rabies in Trinidad transmitted by bats to human beings and the lower animals from 1925. Carib. Med. J. 2(1-4):1-250.

*WATERTON, C. 1925. Wanderings in South America. J. Mawman, London.

*WATKINS, L. C., J. K. JONES, Jr., and H. H. GENOWAYS. 1972. Bats of Jalisco Mexico. Spec. Publ. Mus. Texas Tech Univ. 1:1-44.

*WATSON, E. M. 1991. Television horror movie hosts. McFarland and Co., Jefferson, NC.

*WELLS, J. W. 1886. Exploring and traveling three thousand miles through Brazil from Rio de Janeiro to Maranhao. 2 vols. J. B. Lippincott Co., Philadelphia.

*WILBERT, J., and K. SIMONEAU. 1983. Folk literature of the Bororo Indians. Univ. Calif. Los Angeles Latin American Center Publ., Univ. California.

WILKINSON, G. S. 1984. Reciprocal food sharing in the vampire bat. Nature 308:181.

REFERENCES

*_____. 1985. The social organization of the common vampire bat. Behav. Ecol. Sociobiol. 17:111-134.

_____. 1986. Social grooming in the common vampire bat, *Desmodus rotundus*. Anim. Behav. 34:1880-89.

*_____. 1990. Food sharing in vampire bats. Scien. Amer. Feb.:76-82.

*WILLIAMS, H. E. 1960. Bat transmitted rabies in Trinidad. Can. Vet. J. 1:20-50.

*WILLIAMS, J. J. 1852. The Isthmus of Tehuantepec. D. Appleton and Co., New York.

*WIMSATT, W. A. 1959. Attempted "cannibalism" among captive vampire bats. J. Mammal. 40:439-440.

*_____. 1959. Portrait of a vampire. Ward's Nat. Sci. Bull. 32:35-63.

*_____. 1962. Responses of captive vampires to cold and warm environments. J. Mammal. 43:185-191.

*_____. 1969. Transient behavior, nocturnal activity patterns and feeding efficiency of vampire bats (*Desmodus rotundus*) under natural conditions. J. Mammal. 50:233-244.

*_____. 1978. Vampire bats. *In* Zoo and wild animal medicine, M. E. Fowler, ed., Saunders, Philadelphia.

*WIMSATT, W. A., and A. GUERRIERE. 1961. Care and maintainence of the common vampire bat in captivity. J. Mammal. 42:449-455.

*_____. 1962. Observations on the feeding capacities and excretory functions of captive vampire bats. J. Mammal. 43:17-27.

*WIMSATT, W. A., A. L. GUERRIERE, and R. HORST. 1973. An improved cage design for maintaining vampires (*Desmodus*) and other bats for experimental purposes. J. Mammal. 54:251-254.

WIMSATT, W. A., and H. TRAPIDO. 1952. Reproduction and the female reproductive cycle in the tropical American vampire bat, *Desmodus rotundus rotundus*. Amer. J. Anat. 91:414-446.

*WOLF, L. 1974. Monsters. Straight Arrow Books, San Francisco.

WOOD, J. G. 1869. Illustrated natural history. George Routedge & Sons, London and New York.

*WOODROFFE, J. W. 1914. The upper reaches of the Amazon. MacMillan Co., London.

WRIGHT, D. 1914. Vampires and vampirism. William Rider and Son, Ltd., London. 2nd ed., 1924.

*YOUNG, A. M. 1971. Foraging of vampire bats (*Desmodus rotundus*) in Atlantic wet lowland Costa Rica. Rev. Biol. Trop. 18(1,2):73-88.

ACKNOWLEDGEMENTS

Anyone writing a book on natural history owes a debt to a great many people. For this effort I am especially grateful to my colleagues Randy Babb, Karen Galindo, Pete Mayne and Barry Spicer who helped net and photograph vampire bats in their natural habitat in southern Sonora. That our attempts were successful were due to their never-ceasing enthusiasm and the generous help of Ernesto Alcorn and José Maria Miranda of the Asociación Ganadera Local de Alamos. These dedicated professionals were not only eager to share their extensive knowledge of vampire bat lore and local roost sites, they cheerfully assisted in the bats' capture.

For the all-important technical review of the manuscript I am much indebted to neuro-veterinarian Dan Brass; mammalogist Timothy J. McCarthy at the Carnegie Museum of Natural History in Pittsburgh, Pennsylvania; Quality Control Officer G. Clay Mitchell of the U.S. Animal and Plant Health Inspection Service, Animal Damage Control Program, Denver Wildlife Research Center; and bat biologist Ronnie Sidner at the University of Arizona in Tucson. Not only did these people readily assist me in their respective areas of expertise, they cheerfully corrected my many erroneous statements with patience and kindness. Without these specialists, and the editorial comments of Randy Babb, Neil Carmony, Bruce Hayward, and Barry Spicer, the accuracy and readability of the book would be much diminished.

Special thanks again to Randy Babb, who not only provided the maps and drawings, but many of the photos. Other photos were supplied by Clay Mitchell, Bruce Hayward, and Maureen Haug of the Eastman Kodak Company and are so credited. I am also indebted to Jeffrey S. Arnold, Curatorial Assistant at the University of Michigan's Museum of Zoology, and to Yars Petryszyn, Curator for the Mammal Collection at the University of Arizona, for arranging the loan of hairy-legged and white-winged vampire bat specimens -- thus enabling Randy Babb to use actual animals as models.

Essential administrative and logistical assistance was cheerfully provided by Presidente Concepión Nieblas de Acosta of the Asociación Ganadera local de Alamos in Sonora, Mexico; the Interlibrary Loan staff at Arizona State University in Tempe, Arizona; and the technicians of the Maricopa County Rabies Control Clinic in Phoenix, Arizona.

Thanks too, to Donna Howell, Tim McCarthy, and Patricia Morton for putting me on the trail of some rich literature sources on vampire bat folklore. Also helpful in various ways were Elaine Brown, E. Lendell Cockrum, Denny Constantine, Russell Davis, Angel M. Esquer, Thom Hulen, Terry Johnson, Nancy Lewis, W.L. Minckley, and

Stephanie Myers. Finally, but by no means of lesser importance, I would like to express my appreciation to the rural people of Costa Rica, Honduras, Guatemala, and Mexico who always politely answered my every question no matter how ridiculous. *Hasta la vista.*

143

About the author: A wildlife biologist for 27 years with the Arizona Game and Fish Department, David E. Brown is presently an adjunct professor with the Zoology Department at Arizona State University. Besides working in the American Southwest, he has traveled extensively in Mexico and visited Guatemala, Honduras, Belize, and Costa Rica. He nonetheless considers himself a student of vampire bats, not an expert on them. Brown has authored several books on wildlife including *The Wolf in the Southwest*, (University of Arizona Press), *The Grizzly in the Southwest*, (University of Oklahoma Press), and most recently, *Gila Monster: America's Aztec Lizard* (with Neil Carmony) which is also published by High-Lonesome Books.